Shape A Circle Ever Wider

Liturgical Inculturation in the United States

MARK R. FRANCIS, csv

Foreword by ANSCAR J. CHUPUNGCO, osb

LTP

LITURGY
TRAINING
PUBLICATIONS

Acknowledgments

Quotations from the documents of the Second Vatican Council are from Austin Flannery, ed. *Vatican Council II: The Basic Sixteen Documents.* Northport, New York, 1996.

Excerpts from "Sing a New Church" by Delores Dufner, OSB © 1991 Sisters of St. Benedict. Published by OCP Publications, 5536 NE Hassalo, Portland OR 97213. All rights reserved. Used with permission.

SHAPE A CIRCLE EVER WIDER: LITURGICAL INCULTURATION IN THE UNITED STATES © 2000 Archdiocese of Chicago, Liturgy Training Publications, 1800 North Hermitage Avenue, Chicago IL 60622-1101; 1-800-933-1800; orders@ltp.org; fax 1-800-933-7094. All rights reserved.

Visit our website at www.ltp.org.

This book was edited by David A. Lysik. The production editor was Bryan Cones. The design is by Lucy Smith, and the typesetting was done by Karen Mitchell in Leawood and Futura. This book was printed by Webcom Limited in Toronto, Canada.

04 03 02 01 00   5 4 3 2 1

Library of Congress Cataloging-in-Publication Data

Francis, Mark R.
     Shape a circle ever wider: Liturgical
     inculturation in the United States / Mark R.
     Francis; foreword by Anscar J. Chupungco.
       p. cm.
     Includes bibliographical references.
     ISBN 1-56854-277-1
      1. Catholic Church—United States—Liturgy.
      2. Christianity and culture. I. Title.

  BX1970 .F735 2000
  264'.02'00973—dc21

                   00-038061

CIRCLE

To my colleagues
at Catholic Theological Union—
in thanksgiving for their passion in
serving the plebs sancta Dei

Contents

vi   Foreword
         Anscar J. Chupungco, OSB

xi   Introduction

1   *Chapter One*
         The Relationship of the Church and the World
              The Church and the World from 1200 to 1900
              Effects on the Liturgy
              From Rigidity to Creative Ferment

10   *Chapter Two*
         What Is Culture?
              The Evolving Concept of Culture
              Challenges to the Classicist Notion of Culture
              Culture as a Way of Making Sense out of Life
              Ethnocentrism

20   *Chapter Three*
         The Interplay between Culture
          and Liturgy throughout History
              Inculturation and the First Generation of Believers
              Christians of the Second and Third Centuries
              The "Classical" Roman Rite
              The Germanization of the Church and the Liturgy
              The Missionary Outreach of the
                  Sixteenth and Seventeenth Centuries
              A Record of Inculturation

48 *Chapter Four*
The Process of Liturgical Inculturation
Vatican II: Culture and Liturgy
The Process of Cultural Adaptation of the Liturgy
From Adaptation to Liturgical Inculturation
Creativity
Four Critical Relationships between Liturgy and Culture
The Pastoral Context

78 *Chapter Five*
Inculturation of the Liturgy in the United States
A Look at Culture in the United States
Catholicism and U.S. Culture
Practical Steps toward Inculturation
The Multicultural Social Reality of the United States
Liturgical Inculturation in a Multicultural Context

113 Conclusion

119 Pastoral Resources

Foreword

Anscar J. Chupungco, osb

One of the architects of the reform of the liturgy, Annibale Bugnini, cm, described the work of liturgical reform following the Second Vatican Council as having three stages. The first stage consisted of the use of the vernacular; the second involved the revision of liturgical books; and the third concerned the adaptation of the liturgy to different cultures and traditions. This third stage is better known today as "inculturation."

We all know how wearisome it was for several fathers of the Council to agree to the wider use of the vernacular in the Roman liturgy. For the Roman church, abandoning the venerable Latin prayers in favor of translated texts was as difficult in the twentieth century as it had been in the fourth century to give up using Greek in the liturgy. In effect, translation is a basic form of inculturation. When we translate, we inculturate—unless we settle for a literal translation, which generally fails to capture the message and relay it to the people being addressed. Inculturation favors dynamic equivalence and seems to stress liturgical diversity rather than the uniformity of the Roman rite.

Even the second of Bugnini's stages—the revision of liturgical books—was questioned during the Council. To some Council fathers the word "revision" was threatening. For centuries, the Roman church had been using the same books. Why change them now? Was there anything wrong with them? Yet the underpinning principle of the reform of the liturgy was (and is) that revision must take into account not only the historical development of the rite but also the present situation of the church. The revision of liturgical books is in great part a work of inculturation. Furthermore, the revised books are called *editiones typicae.* This means that they are basically *models* to be used by the national conferences of bishops to produce liturgical books for their respective local churches. Once again, we are dealing with inculturation. To celebrate the liturgy exactly as the *editio typica* describes it, without consideration of the local culture and context, is to miss the point of the conciliar reform.

Having accepted the use of the vernacular and the revision of the liturgical books, the Council fathers did not have much problem approving articles 37–40 of the Constitution on the Liturgy *Sacrosanctum concilium.* These articles deal with inculturation—the third stage of the renewal of the liturgy. In other words, the third stage of the post-conciliar reform should flow effortlessly from the previous stages. We know, however, that this has not been the case. Articles 37–40 had to be studied exegetically, and the principles and norms of inculturation had to be specified. The comforting thing is that a good deal of work was done during the years following the Council. Articles and books were published, conferences and study weeks were held, and the faithful were alerted to the possible effects of inculturation. Indeed, several attempts were made to give concrete shape to the principles of inculturation. The episcopal conference of India, followed by those of Zaire and the Philippines, integrated local cultural expressions into the eucharistic liturgy of the Roman rite. The efforts of the conferences of India and Zaire toward inculturated liturgies even received official recognition from Rome.

In 1994 the Vatican Congregation for Divine Worship and the Discipline of the Sacraments issued the instruction *Varietates legitimae* (Inculturation and the Roman Liturgy). Although the aim of the document is to offer practical guidelines, its understanding of inculturation remains very much within established historical theological parameters. In fact, it fails to address the basic question of methodology.

In short, the topic of inculturation still has many loose ends. The Vatican instruction has by no means put the finishing touches to it, although some sectors of the church want to believe that there is nothing more to add to the instruction. More disheartening is the attitude of those pastors and faithful who regard inculturation as a dead issue: "All we need now are good translations of the *editiones typicae* of the liturgical books!" By "good translations" some mean *literal* translations, thus effectively deleting the item of inculturation from the post-conciliar agenda.

This new book by Mark Francis comes at a time when it has become necessary to reaffirm the agenda of the Second Vatican Council, which prominently includes the question of liturgical inculturation. He narrates the bored and frustrated reaction of a Presbyterian seminarian from Virginia toward inculturation, and we know that seminarian is not alone in his boredom and frustration. There are a number of Roman Catholics who feel the same way and speak their feelings aloud. This book, whose intended readership includes members of parish liturgy committees, pastoral ministers, seminarians and students of liturgy and theology, is a welcome contribution to the continuing work of liturgical reform through inculturation.

In his conclusion, Mark—whom I have called by his first name since his days as a student—writes, "The purpose of this book was to examine how a living tradition of worship such as the Roman rite might be adapted to speak more eloquently the gospel of Jesus Christ to the culturally diverse peoples of the United States." A former student and now a colleague of mine, Mark shares fully what I have always taught: Inculturation is a serious business. Although it is a creative endeavor, it also demands that we build on the existing structures of the tradition of worship enshrined in the

Roman liturgy. Furthermore, it requires us to establish principles and norms, and to identify possibilities and options. That is how serious inculturation is.

Mark's first four chapters are all about this tedious but necessary area of inculturation. These chapters serve as an indispensable introduction, and the reader should not skip them. Their aim is to lead the reader to the fifth chapter, in which Mark discusses the cultural reality of the United States and how it can be supportive of liturgical worship.

Although I have tinkered with applied inculturation for the Philippines—I have never dared to do so in Italy, where I lived for 24 years—including the Mass and the Rite of Marriage, my writings have been chiefly in the area of general principles and norms. What is required at this point is a serious study of the traditions and cultural patterns of local churches. We need to define such patterns if we want to give concrete shape to the principles and norms of liturgical inculturation. We should know not only what we are inculturating (the Roman liturgy) but also the context in which we inculturate (local traditions and cultures).

This phase can be very frustrating, especially when the local culture is multicultural. In this day and age, there are perhaps very few countries with only a single culture. Even in such places, the cultural stratum or common culture is usually diversified by sub-cultures. Multiculturalism is the reality in most of our world today. But multiculturalism applies with special force to the United States, which embraces a variety of ethnic traditions and cultures. To define the United States as one culture would be unrealistic if not damaging to the future of liturgical reform in this country. I should note that in 1991 Mark published his important work *Liturgy in a Multicultural Community*. The problem, it seems, has been haunting Mark for at least a decade.

The fifth chapter of Mark's book should be read in the context of the preceding chapters. Its thrust is clearly to examine with the reader the gamut of issues and areas covered by inculturation: gesture and posture, environment and art, areas for devotion, verbal communication, music, and the liturgical calendar. All these liturgical "facts" need to be studied in light of the cultural or multicultural contexts of the United States. Mark names these contexts, defines them, and shows how they can influence the liturgical "facts." The contexts include popular religiosity, which is alive in the United States but tends to become an increasingly private affair, and "megachurches," which are, for good or ill, a response to U.S. culture. Other aspects of the U.S. cultural context are postmodernity, the issue of the dignity of the human person, the question of feminism, and concern for the marginalized. These are some of the cultural patterns Mark has identified, and in light them he offers a host of possibilities and options for liturgical inculturation. The reader might be overwhelmed by the vastness of it all but will surely be grateful to be led with a feeling of security in an undertaking as complex and delicate as liturgical inculturation.

I thank Mark for saying that my name "is now synonymous with liturgical inculturation." That might be so in the broad sense—in the arena of norms and general principles of inculturation—but not in the concrete situations of local churches. The names that are synonymous with inculturation in this latter context are of people who work to implement the general principles and norms. Thus, I accept Mark's compliment with the conviction that it needs to be joined with compliments to all those involved with inculturation on the local scene. In the United States, one such person is Mark Francis himself.

Introduction

Several years ago I was having a conversation about liturgy with an ecumenical group of students, and the topic of culture came up. Since I was the only one of the group who had ever lived outside the United States, I spoke of my experiences as a Roman Catholic who had worshiped in places as different as Hong Kong, Colombia and Italy. I tried to describe how the cultural background of the people in each of these settings influenced the way the Roman rite of Mass was celebrated and experienced. One member of the group, a young Presbyterian seminarian from Virginia, seemed rather frustrated with the conversation. He mentioned that while all this was interesting, it had no applicability to his experience. He explained that there was very little diversity in his part of the country, where practically everyone he knew was white, middle class and Protestant. He finally said in an exasperated tone, "You're talking about all these people with cultures. I'm from Roanoke. . . . I have no culture!"

His comment was telling. My friend from Roanoke was convinced that because he did not recognize any cultural influence in the way he worshiped, he was somehow "culture-free." The group had an excellent exchange at that point, during which we discussed the tendency that all human beings have of equating their way of doing something with the "standard" or "normal" way, while regarding any difference in language or custom as "ethnic" or "cultural." The fact is that we all are influenced by the particular culture we have been brought up in, and by the values and points of view passed on to us by our families, schools and churches.

Why a book on inculturating the Roman Catholic liturgy in the United States? Isn't inculturation something that is done in mission lands, with and by people who are newly evangelized? Why would the Roman rite need to be inculturated in a country like the United States, which is heir to Western cultural traditions? To my mind, these questions reflect an attitude very similar to that of the student from Roanoke. They fail to take into account the influence "mainstream" middle-class U.S. culture has on our interpretation and celebration of the received liturgical tradition. Those who have attended Mass around the United States know that liturgical style, music and gesture can vary a great deal, even between European American middle-class churches. Parish liturgies in the various geographical regions of the country exhibit different styles or tones that are not just occasioned by the eccentricities of the priest or a particular parish liturgy committee.

The following pages will present a reflection on the elements that come into play when we place our liturgical tradition in dialogue with the rich and variegated cultural reality of the United States. While there has been much written on the topic of liturgical inculturation from an international perspective,[1] far less has been written from the perspective of U.S. culture and worship. This book is written for students of liturgy and theology, as well as those who serve on liturgy committees or are engaged in parish adult education. For that reason, I have tried to keep technical language to a minimum but have chosen to place references to more scholarly works in endnotes. This volume is meant to be introductory and primarily pastoral—and I make no pretensions that it is an exhaustive treatment of a topic as complex as the relationship between culture and liturgy. This book is simply the product of my research and teaching in the nearly twelve years since my studies in Rome with Father Anscar Chupungco, OSB, whose name is now synonymous with liturgical inculturation. Local churches around the world owe him a debt of gratitude for his work. I add my personal appreciation and thanks for his groundbreaking scholarship and his ongoing ministry as founder and director of the Paul VI Liturgical

Institute in Malaybalay City, Philippines. My academic life since Rome has been richly blessed by my colleagues at Catholic Theological Union in Chicago, where issues surrounding culture and theology are a constant topic of formal and informal conversation.

This book is arranged in five chapters and a conclusion; each will treat particular issues concerning liturgy and culture. The first chapter sets the scene and describes the church's renewed understanding of its relationship with the world, which is expressed in the documents of the Second Vatican Council. The second chapter discusses the rich and complex phenomenon of human culture, from a definition anchored in European values, philosophy and art forms, to a more current, relative understanding.

Chapter three offers a sketch of some of the ways that the liturgy has been transformed by the cultures into which the church has moved over the centuries. Chapter four looks at the process of liturgical inculturation set in motion by Vatican II and suggests various interpretive perspectives through which to view this process today, more than thirty years after the Council. In this examination we will be especially interested in how our liturgical and ritual heritage has been and could be transformed or reinterpreted as it moves into different cultures.

Chapter five discusses the cultural reality of the United States and how this context affects liturgy. Acknowledging that U.S. culture is both complex and multicultural, the chapter explores the "mainstream" U.S. culture formed by the European American groups with an eye to the cultural diversity inherent in the U.S. experience as a nation of immigrants. What are the characteristics of U.S. society that challenge liturgical worship? How can characteristics of our culture also be supportive of worship? This is followed by a discussion of the inculturation of the different liturgical "languages," or ways in which the liturgy communicates:

gesture and posture, environment and art, devotional areas, verbal communication, music, and time.

Chapter five also explores multicultural liturgy. The challenge of welcoming people from diverse cultural backgrounds into one liturgy is new to the Roman rite, and the response of the church in the United States places it in the international forefront. Residents of the United States in practically every region of the country increasingly come into contact with people from a wide range of cultural traditions: Hispanic, Asian, African American, African, South Pacific and Middle Eastern. This contact inevitably changes our lives. Because liturgy is a living expression of the faith, this context must also affect the way we worship.

The conclusion sums up and builds upon the previous chapters by offering some reflections on the future of Roman Catholic liturgy in the United States. Inculturation of worship is ultimately about helping make the good news of Jesus Christ as expressed in our liturgical tradition understandable and accessible to our brothers and sisters. Benedictine Sister Delores Dufner, in the last two verses and refrain of her wonderful hymn "Sing a New Church," sums up our task:

> Bring the hopes of ev'ry nation;
> Bring the art of ev'ry race.
> Weave a song of peace and justice;
> Let it sound through time and space.
>
> Draw together at one table
> All the human family;
> Shape a circle ever wider
> And a people ever free.
>
> Let us bring the gifts that differ
> And, in splendid, varied ways,
> Sing a new church into being,
> One in faith and love and praise.[2]

Inculturation is a challenge to explore the most faithful way of continuing the work of the Second Vatican Council—to constructively engage the world with the good news of Jesus Christ and so shape a circle ever wider.

July 31, 1999
Memorial of Saint Ignatius of Loyola

Notes

1. The international authority on liturgical inculturation is Anscar Chupungco, OSB, former president of the Pontifical Liturgical Institute of Sant' Anselmo in Rome. His major works on this topic are *Cultural Adaptation of the Liturgy* (New York: Paulist Press, 1982); *Liturgies of the Future* (New York: Paulist Press, 1989); *Liturgical Inculturation: Sacramentals, Religiosity and Catechesis* (Collegeville, Minnesota: The Liturgical Press, 1992); and *Worship: Sound Tradition and Legitimate Progress* (Washington, D.C.: The Pastoral Press, 1994).

2. Delores Dufner, OSB, "Sing a New Church," (Portland, Oregon: OCP Publications, 1991).

Chapter One

The Relationship of the Church and the World

The face of the Catholic church in the United States is changing dramatically. From a church made up of predominantly urban, working-class European immigrants at the beginning of the twentieth century, parishes today throughout the country are becoming increasingly more diverse. Many of the descendants of the European immigrants who came to these shores in the early 1900s are educated men and women who have "made it" socially and economically, and now occupy positions of responsibility and privilege in the upper echelons of American business, academia and medicine. But the marginalized Catholic immigrant is still very much a part of the church. Largely Hispanic and Asian, the new immigrants are steadily becoming a majority in the same neighborhoods originally inhabited by European American Catholics. African American Catholics, long a group shamefully ignored by church leaders, are also assuming a presence and exerting a witness that can no longer be overlooked. When examining the Catholic presence in the United States, never have the famous words of James Joyce describing the church been more accurate: "Here comes everybody."

What does any of this have to do with the liturgy? These demo-graphic changes in and of themselves might not have had any effect on how we Roman Catholics gather for worship if it were not for the revolutionary impact of the Second Vatican Council (1962–65). The reform of the liturgy mandated by Vatican II invited Catholics to enter into worship with a renewed vision of the church's relationship with the world. In the first sentence of the Pastoral Constitution on the Church in the Modern World *Gaudium et spes,* the last document issued by Vatican II, the fathers of the Council eloquently announced the church's reengagement with the world: "The joys and hopes, the grief and anguish of the people of our time, especially of those who are poor or afflicted, are the joys and hopes, the grief and anguish of the followers of Christ as well" (#1). The Council presupposes that the church does not operate in some sphere disengaged from humanity, but has the responsibility of "reading the signs of the times and of interpreting them in the light of the Gospel" (#4).

The liturgical assembly—seen by the Council as the manifesta-tion of the church in a particular place and time—must in some way bring the joy and hope, the pain and anguish of the world to its wor-ship. In many ways, this was the principal goal of the liturgical reform. More than a simple rearrangement of furniture (moving the altar away from the wall), the rites as revised by Vatican II reflect the ecclesiology (the theology of church) articulated in the documents of the Council. This ecclesiology, announced in the first document of the Council, the Constitution on the Sacred Liturgy *Sacrosanctum concilium,* and developed in the Dogmatic Constitution on the Church *Lumen gentium,* moved away from an exclusively hierarchical view of the church. The church, while hierarchically organized, is first presented through the biblical image of the people of God, a priestly community, which, when celebrating the eucharist, most fully realizes its identity as the Body of Christ in the world.[1] The vision advanced by Vatican II proposes a very different relationship between the church and the secular world than held sway during the preceding 400 years. It is significant that the guiding principle of the

Council was expressed with the Italian word *aggiornamento,* "bringing the church up to date" or "into dialogue" with the times and the surrounding cultures in which Christians live.

This dialogue with the world necessarily opened the church's worship to the influence of local cultures. In fact, this relationship between the faith and its cultural expression has been a consistent area of concern for both Pope Paul VI and Pope John Paul II because of its obvious implications for both evangelization and liturgy. In his groundbreaking encyclical on evangelization *Evangelii nuntiandi* (1975), Paul VI urgently points out that "the split between the Gospel and culture is without a doubt the drama of our time, just as it was of other times. Therefore every effort must be made to ensure a full evangelization of culture, or more correctly of cultures" (#20).

It is important to note that this concern for a conscious dialogue with cultures on the part of the church is relatively recent. We are still learning how to carry on this dialogue more than 30 years after the close of the Council, primarily because the church had not been on serious speaking terms with culture since the Middle Ages.

The Church and the World from 1200 to 1900

The Second Vatican Council's call for dialogue and "updating" marked a radical departure from the way Roman Catholics understood the relationship of faith to Western culture. To appreciate how revolutionary the idea of *aggiornamento* was, it is useful to examine briefly the history of the church's attitude toward the secular world since the thirteenth century.

It is significant that some historians call the thirteenth century the "age of faith."[2] At that time, Western European culture was essentially synonymous with Catholic Christianity. Medieval music, art and architecture were all imbued with Christian forms and symbols. Political treaties between nations were signed in the name of the Trinity. Philosophy and science were considered "handmaids" to theological inquiry. But this medieval synthesis had broken down by the fifteenth and sixteenth centuries. The Renaissance and the Reformation challenged the central position held by theology in interpreting life for people of western Europe. This is seen most clearly in Western philosophy, which gradually distanced itself from theology and moved toward a rationalism that became increasingly wary of making absolute claims about truth, especially when those claims were expressed in religious language.[3]

From the time of the Council of Trent (1545–63), the church considered itself challenged and even threatened by modern trends in philosophy, science and politics—all of which were viewed as hostile to the traditional understanding of the faith as expressed in both doctrinal definitions and worship. Beginning in the seventeenth century, scientific discoveries about the physical world changed the medieval conception of the universe by placing the sun rather than the earth (and humanity) in the center of the solar system—a view initially contested by church authorities. Finally, the development of representative democracy in the eighteenth and nineteenth centuries was looked upon by the church with suspicion as an unwarranted departure from the rule of Christian kings duly anointed by the church and charged by God to rule their subjects and maintain the faith in their realms.

Feeling vulnerable because of these challenges, the church saw its role as one of protecting and preserving the faith against the errors of the modern world. There was little room for dialogue with the surrounding cultures, since by definition they were in error and in need of the church's enlightenment. This antagonism of the church toward the modern world reached its most systematic articulation in Pope Pius IX's condemnation of 80 "modern ideas," including the freedom of religion and the separation of church and state, in his *Syllabus of Errors,* issued in 1864.

Effects on the Liturgy

Not surprisingly, the celebration of the liturgy during the centuries after the Council of Trent reflected this lack of dialogue between the church and the world.[4] In response to many of the abuses that occasioned the Reformation, the Council of Trent gave the Roman Curia the task of overseeing the liturgy and safeguarding it from error. The rite of Mass promulgated under the authority of Pius V in 1570 proposed what was essentially a form of celebration dating from the late Middle Ages, but shorn of abuses. This form of the rite (also known as the Tridentine rite, named after the Council of Trent) became the standard way the Roman rite was celebrated in all parts of the Catholic world for the next 400 years. Papal regulations prescribed that this Roman rite should everywhere form the basis of all worship, except in those places that had their own liturgies for more than 200 years prior. Any additions or alterations to the liturgy were to be exclusively reserved to the Holy See. Because of the insistence on following the ritual prescriptions of the liturgical books, many historians of worship characterize this period as "the age of rubricism."[5]

Ironically, this level of enforced standardization, previously unknown in the history of the Roman rite, was made possible by the relatively new technology of the printing press; exact copies of the standardized rites could be printed and made obligatory in the Catholic world. In order to enforce the rubrics established by the Holy See, the priest was given detailed instructions on exactly what do to at every moment of the Mass. In the introductory section to the Tridentine missal, after the general rubrics and norms governing the calendar, an even more detailed section entitled *Ritus servandus in celebratione missae* (the rites to be used in celebrating the Mass) was followed by an exhaustive and legalistic listing of the *De defectibus*, or defects, that could occur at Mass, some of which could affect the validity of the celebration and cause the priest to commit not only venial but mortal sin.[6]

The uniform rite of Mass itself was held up by Catholic apologists as a monument to the timelessness and universality of the Catholic faith. It was said that you could go anywhere in the world and the Mass would be celebrated in exactly the same way. From Beijing to Botswana, from Paris to Peoria, the Mass was supposed to be identical. While this assertion was exaggerated, the important part of the rite—the part done by the priest—was invariable. Ideally, the customs and culture of the people attending the Mass had absolutely no influence; the rubrics were determined beforehand in Rome and were to be scrupulously observed.

This rite reflected an ecclesiology that emphasized the mediation of the priest and gave a secondary role to the assembly. The physical distance between the faithful and the celebrant was significant. The priest celebrated at an altar located at the far end of the church within a "sanctuary" cordoned off by a communion rail. He celebrated inaudibly in Latin with his back to the people, giving the impression that the Mass was a clerical prerogative. The presence of lay people in the celebration—at least from the canonical point of view—was of secondary importance, and quite optional. It is interesting to note that in the highly-detailed rubrics in the introductory material of the Tridentine missal, the role of the assembly—the lay people in attendance—is not even mentioned.[7]

Thus, the uniform rite of Mass issued by Pius V—clerical, rubrically detailed, invariable in execution and rigidly enforced—became the hallmark of Counter-Reformation Catholicism in the Roman rite. Consistent with the church's negative and defensive attitude toward the ideas and cultural developments of the surrounding world, the central parts of the Mass and other liturgies of the church were largely untouched by local cultural influences for almost 400 years.

From Rigidity to Creative Ferment

This state of affairs was challenged in the early 1900s by scholars and pastors who sought to return the liturgy to what its etymology suggests: "a work of the people." Inspired by the work of the international liturgical movement, which began some fifty years before the Council,[8] the first document of Vatican II, the Constitution on the Sacred Liturgy *Sacrosanctum concilium* (SC), radically changed the Tridentine understanding and practice of the liturgy. Roman Catholic worship was no longer regarded as a set of rubrics to be duly performed by those in holy orders. In the words of the Council, "Pastors of souls must, therefore, realize that, when the liturgy is celebrated, their obligation goes further than simply ensuring that the laws governing valid and lawful celebration are observed" (SC, 11). Henceforth the liturgy was not considered the sole domain of clerical specialists but was understood to belong to all the faithful by virtue of their baptism. The overarching aim of the entire liturgical reform was clearly announced in article 14 of the liturgy constitution: "It is very much the wish of the church that all the faithful should be led to take that full, conscious and active part in liturgical celebrations which is demanded by the very nature of the liturgy."

Clearly, the participation envisioned by the Council depends on the ability of our rites to communicate meaningfully to the members of the assembly gathered in Christ's name. For this reason, people charged with the pastoral work of preparing liturgical celebrations are encouraged by the conciliar and post-conciliar documents to take into account the people who gather for the celebration. For example, the *General Instruction of the Roman Missal* states that "the pastoral effectiveness of a celebration will be heightened if the texts of readings, prayers and songs correspond as closely as possible to the needs, religious dispositions, and aptitude of the participants" (#313). This is a dramatic departure from the unchangeable and rigid Tridentine directives, which completely ignored the people in the pews.

The pastoral consideration of preparing the rites in light of the needs, religious dispositions and aptitude of the members of the assembly is the basis for what we today call the "inculturation" of the liturgy. Liturgical inculturation has as its aim seeing to it that the members of the assembly take their "full, conscious, and active part" in liturgical celebrations. Attentiveness to the culture (and cultures) of the members of the local church, then, is essential if worship is to communicate the good news of Jesus Christ in an effective way. At heart it is a matter of evangelization. As Paul VI notes in *Evangelii nuntiandi,* "Evangelization loses much of its force and effectiveness if it does not take into consideration the actual people to whom it is addressed, if it does not use their language, their signs and symbols, if it does not answer the questions they ask, and if it does not have an impact on their concrete life" (#63). In order to take into consideration the "actual people" at worship, we turn now to a study of culture since, as the Second Vatican Council observed, "[i]t is a feature of the human person that it can achieve true and full humanity only by means of culture" (*Gaudium et spes,* 53).

Notes

1. See especially *Sacrosanctum concilium,* 10, and *Lumen gentium,* 11, and Nathan Mitchell, "Liturgy and Ecclesiology," and Mark R. Francis, "The Liturgical Assembly," in A. Chupungco, ed., *Handbook for Liturgical Studies II* (Collegeville, Minnesota: The Liturgical Press, 1998), 113–44. For an ecumenical perspective see Gordon Lathrop, *Holy People: A Liturgical Ecclesiology* (Minneapolis: Augsburg Fortress Press, 1999), 21–48.

2. This term was popularized by Will and Ariel Durant in their multi-volume overview of Western history.

3. Pope John Paul II's encyclicals *Veritatis splendor* and *Fides et ratio* describe the chasm that developed between philosophy and theology in the West. Both of these encyclicals call for philosophy and theology to search for truth in ways proper to each discipline.

4. For a history of the Roman rite after the Council of Trent, see Theodor Klauser, *A Short History of the Western Liturgy: An Account and Some Reflections* (London: Oxford University Press, 1979), 117–52.

5. *Ibid.,* 117–135; Enrico Cattaneo, *Il culto cristano in occidente. Note storiche* (Roma: C.L.V. Edizioni Liturgiche, 1978), 360–78.

6. For a comparison of this document with the present introduction to the Roman Missal, see Burckhard Neunheuser, "The Relation of Priest and Faithful in the Liturgies of Pius V and Paul VI," *Roles in the Liturgical Assembly* (New York: Pueblo, 1981), 207–19; Frederick McManus, "From *Rubricae generales* and *Ritus servandus* to *Institutio generalis,*" in K. Hughes, ed., *Finding Voice to Give God Praise* (Collegeville, Minnesota: The Liturgical Press, 1998), 214–42.

7. It is also interesting to note, however, that the assembly was mentioned in the rubrics of the 1474 missal that was the forerunner to the Tridentine missal of 1570. The changed ecclesial climate brought on by the Reformeration insistence that the eucharist was a communal celebration seemed to harden the Roman position, which emphasized the role of the priest and ignored that of the laity. See Adrien Nocent, *La messa prima e dopo San Pio V* (Casale Monferrato: Piemme, 1985).

8. On the liturgical movement, especially its connection to social justice and other contemporary issues, see Keith F. Pecklers, *The Unread Vision: The Liturgical Movement in the United States of America: 1926–1955* (Collegeville, Minnesota: The Liturgical Press, 1998).

Chapter Two

What Is Culture?

An understanding of culture is necessary before any effort is made to inculturate the liturgy. But this is not as easy as it may look at first glance. "Culture" is often used to describe various, sometimes contradictory realities. In the 1950s scholars discussed 164 different definitions of this term in modern English.[1] From "education" or "refinement" to more technical definitions developed by sociologists and anthropologists, there are few other words in the English language with so many connotations. The reason for this is simple: Western thinking about culture has evolved a great deal over the last 200 years, and it is still evolving due to the increasing effects of globalization.[2] This evolving understanding of culture has also affected how the church understands itself and presents its message. For this reason, it is useful to begin our discussion of inculturation with an overview of the meanings and nuances of this complex concept.

The Evolving Concept of Culture

Prior to the advent of the social sciences at the beginning of the twentieth century, the word "culture"—at least as it was popularly used in Europe and North America—was synonymous with the achievements of Western European civilization: the art and philosophy of Greece; the law and architecture of ancient Rome; the works of such writers as Shakespeare, Goethe and Molière; the art of Michaelangelo, Rubens and Monet; the music of Bach, Mozart and Brahms. Familiarity with such as these indicated that one was "cultured." The institutions, philosophies and works of art created by Europeans formed the Western "canon," or accepted list of what people needed to know in order to consider themselves "cultured." Even today, people who spend time at the opera or the art museum are often referred to as "culture vultures." These cultured few are sometimes contrasted to the majority of people who lack formal higher education and are described as "low brow," "vulgar" or "unrefined."

It is instructive to look at how our society regards education as the primary way of passing down the common values and assumptions about life, or cultural identity, that distinguishes a citizen of the United States from a citizen of another nation. School boards charged with establishing curriculum standards necessarily have to wrestle with what constitutes the cultural core of our national identity. One of their functions is to promote through education what they have identified as U.S. values and traditions. Respect for democracy, some knowledge of U.S. history and of our constitutional system of government, and a working knowledge of English are considered the prerequisites for being a good citizen. This forms a basic part of the curriculum in elementary schools throughout the country. In this sense U.S. civic culture goes beyond ethnic groups and serves as a canopy under which people of diverse national backgrounds can take refuge.

The concern to pass on this cultural core, however, takes on other dimensions at higher levels of education. For example, the curricular "culture wars" currently being fought in universities and on school boards across the country usually pit those who hold that Western European cultural achievements are normative and necessary for every educated person against those who opt for a set of course requirements that goes beyond the established canon of Western European and U.S. classics.[3]

The first group, represented by many in the academy and in government, forcefully argue that the United States is heir to the Western European traditions of government, scientific inquiry and the arts, and that it is necessary to pass these traditions on to future generations in order to maintain U.S. cultural identity. Indeed, some argue that our survival as a nation depends on it. Usually this argument is supported by the contention that the United States is a nation steeped in the Judeo-Christian tradition—meaning the form the tradition took in Western Europe.

The second group argues just as forcefully that knowledge of non-European traditions and cultural achievements is also important, especially since many U.S. citizens and residents trace their heritage to parts of the world outside white Europe. While *Beowulf* is an important piece of English literature, for example, so also are the achievements of African, Asian and Hispanic/Latino authors, who are writing of their experiences. Space in the curriculum should therefore be allotted for the study of these works. In addition, given the growing number of diverse ethnic and religious groups in the United States, this group argues that we need to be more inclusive of the religious traditions of people who are not Jewish or Christian.

Both perspectives on the "culture wars" have validity. But it is helpful first of all to discuss assumptions about culture, since these assumptions also influence how Christians make decisions on a host of issues affecting their lives and the workings of society's institutions. Theologian Bernard Lonergan has labeled the traditional assumption about the normativity and superiority of Western civilization as the "classicist" understanding of culture.

> In the older view, culture was conceived not empirically, but normatively. It was the opposite of barbarism. It was a matter of acquiring tastes and skills, the ideals, virtues and ideas, that were pressed upon one in a good home and through a curriculum in the liberal arts. It stressed not facts but values. It could not but claim to be universalist. Its classics were immortal works of art, its philosophy was the perennial philosophy, its laws and structures were the deposit of wisdom and the prudence of

mankind. Classicist education was a matter of models to be imitated, of ideal characters to be emulated, of eternal verities and universal laws. It sought to produce not the mere specialist but the *uomo universale* that could turn his hand to anything and do it brilliantly.[4]

It is hard to underestimate the effect this understanding of culture had on the church in the era prior to Vatican II.[5] Concepts such as religion, education and civilization were regarded as various facets of the same reality. Hilaire Belloc's aphorism "The Faith is Europe and Europe is the Faith" sums up this view.[6] According to this understanding, the duty of the church was to bring its sons and daughters out of ignorance and irreligion and into the light of gospel. This light was Christian European culture and civilization as interpreted by the church—shorn of the rationalism and skepticism of the centuries following the Middle Ages. The European culture that the church championed around the world was essentially a kind of romantic reconstruction of a particular period in European history when the church spoke for the culture.

A book popular in Catholic circles at the beginning of the century and widely distributed by the Knights of Columbus identified this golden age of Christian history: *The Thirteenth, Greatest of Centuries.*[7] This was the "age of faith," the time of the great scholastic synthesis of theology and philosophy, of soaring Gothic cathedrals, of a harmonious fusion of church and state, of universal acceptance of the truths espoused by the church. Of course, the reality of medieval Europe was much less ideal. Yet this romantic view of the Middle Ages inspired generations of Catholics in the nineteenth and twentieth centuries, and served as a unifying vision for what could be called "Catholic culture."

But, as Lonergan points out, not everyone could aspire to be fully initiated into this culture; much depended on individual talent and enterprise. Culture in this sense was for the select few who had the training and intellect to acquire it. Some would have the knowledge; others would be perpetually less learned, less initiated.

On classicist assumptions there is just one culture. That one culture is not attained by the simple faithful, the people, the natives, the barbarians. Nonetheless, career is always open to talent. One enters upon such a career by the diligent study of the ancient Latin and Greek authors. One pursues such a career by learning Scholastic philosophy and theology. One aims at high office by becoming proficient in canon law. One succeeds by winning approbation and favour of the right personages. Within this set-up the unity of faith is a matter of everyone subscribing to the correct formulae.[8]

Challenges to the Classicist Notion of Culture

This elitist and propositional understanding of culture and faith was challenged toward the end of the nineteenth century by the newly-developing social sciences. The often unconscious Christian presumption that Western cultural achievements were somehow universal and normative was also called into question by Europeans and Americans who were more sensitive to non-Western cultures and religious traditions. In the wake of a colonialism that sought to impose European standards on peoples throughout the globe, the observations of field anthropologists and Christian missionaries living in non-Western cultures disputed the normativity and superiority of Western culture.[9]

Prior to Vatican II, however, the church's efforts at evangelization were very much linked to the diffusion of Western culture. In short, European culture was often confused with the gospel itself. This was not only true for the missionary endeavors of the Catholic church, but was true as well for Protestant and evangelical Christians, who brought their particular interpretations of Western culture along with the gospel. One of the early scenes in the movie based on James Michener's novel *Hawaii* illustrates this point well. Calvinist missionaries from New England, in their zeal to preach the gospel and because their sense of decency was offended, set out to dress the almost-naked Hawaiians in European-style clothing.

In a way, for non-European converts to Christianity—both Catholic and Protestant—to become Christian was tantamount to wearing foreign clothes. Conversion meant denying one's culture. There is a saying in Mandarin that dates from the period of early missionary work in Asia: "One more Christian, one less Chinese." As theologian Karl Rahner succinctly describes both Catholic and Protestant missionary efforts in the nineteenth century,

> the actual concrete activity of the Church in its relation to the world outside of Europe was in fact (if you will pardon the expression) the activity of an export firm which exported a European religion as a commodity it did not really want to change but sent throughout the world together with the rest of the culture and civilization it considered superior.[10]

Culture as a Way of Making Sense out of Life

It was only during the twentieth century that the common understanding of culture began to shift. Rather than being synonymous with knowledge of European artistic and scientific achievements, "culture" gradually came to refer to how every human being makes sense out of life individually and as a member of society. In a definition that has now become classic, anthropologist Clifford Geertz describes culture as "a system of inherited conceptions expressed in symbolic forms by means of which human beings communicate, perpetuate and develop their knowledge about, and their attitudes toward, life."[11]

This carefully-worded description deserves some comment. First, Geertz describes culture as "a system of inherited conceptions." Culture has much to do with what we have learned from our parents and others about what it means to be a human being. The totality of the values, ways of acting and understanding that we learned "at our mother's knee," helps us to know how we fit into the world. As we grow up, we learn our culture's general assumptions about family relationships, the relationship between men and women in society,

15

and attitudes toward sexuality and death. In short, culture teaches us our place in the universe. These values and assumptions are most often expressed in day-to-day behavior: how we greet and take leave of one another, table manners, and other conventional ways of acting that express cultural values and assumptions.

Anthropologists refer to growing up in a culture—appropriating the values held by our parents and those who teach us "our way" in the world—as *en*culturation (note that this is not exactly the same as *in*culturation, which will be explained in more detail in chapter four). Enculturation is a process of learning about our home culture; it is not automatic, genetic or inherited. For example, a girl born to Chinese parents in Shanghai but adopted as an infant and raised by an Irish American couple in Boston will be culturally Irish American, even though she may appear to be racially Asian. In other words, culture and race are two different human characteristics: One is learned, the other is genetic.

Another aspect of Geertz's definition is that cultural concepts are expressed in symbolic forms. The most obvious symbolic form is language—the words we use to communicate with one another. No one learns one's mother tongue in a classroom. We learn how to speak and acquire the basic ability to communicate from those who care for us from infancy. Contained in the structure and vocabulary of language are values and attitudes toward the world that we unconsciously assume to be true. For example, in Romance languages such as French and Spanish, mistakes are not completely ascribed to the person in error. In English, we accuse someone who is mistaken by saying, "You *are* wrong!" In French, on the other hand, one says, *"Tu as tort"* (literally, "You *have* wrong"); in French, the condition of being wrong is something one can have but easily discard. If a Spanish-speaking child drops and breaks a dish, her culpability is attenuated by the very way she recounts the accident: *"Se me cayó y se me rompió el plato!"* (The *plate*—in my possession—fell and broke.) This is quite different from the English-speaking child's confession: *"I dropped the plate and broke it!"*

Language, as one of the primary ways we communicate, not only expresses and inculcates values but also enables us to see the world in a certain way. It shapes how we interact with our environment and make sense out of our world. The language of the Inuit—the Native Americans of Alaska—for example, has over 20 different words for "snow," depending on its texture, quality and color. This is not surprising given the environment in which the Inuit live. Because of their rich snow, vocabulary, they are able to recognize and communicate knowledge about snow that would baffle speakers of English. We will see how important the choice of words is when we discuss the question of translation and the language of prayer, since the way we call upon God and address one another expresses our understanding of our relationships with one another and the image of the God we worship.

Language, though, is far from the only symbolic form we use to communicate with one another. We express our cultural values in a variety of "languages": music, dance and gesture; the design and decoration of our homes, churches and workplaces; the ways we greet and take leave of one another; the ways we marry, name children, and bury the dead. These symbolic forms of communication will become important references for us when we consider the process of liturgical inculturation in chapter four.

Ethnocentrism

Because of the way all human beings are enculturated, we have a tendency toward what is called "ethnocentrism"—interpreting and judging all human experience in light of our own cultural values. If people of other cultures do not act as we think they should in a given situation, if they do not share our values and support our particular views—even if they do not look like us—we have a tendency to dismiss them as being both mistaken and inferior. This tendency is well illustrated by an example offered by Father Louis Luzbetak.

> There is the story told of the Anglo-American couple who on
> Memorial Day brought some flowers to the grave of their loved
> ones. They were surprised to see how some Chicanos laid food
> on the graves instead. Surprised, if not amused, they approached
> the Chicanos and asked them, "When do you expect your departed
> to come and eat your food?" Without even looking up, one of
> the Chicanos replied very nonchalantly, "O, about the same time
> your loved ones will come up to smell your flowers."[12]

Living in the multicultural context of the United States, it is crucial
for the well-being of both church and society that we develop a sensitivity to and respect for the customs and traditions of others. That is
not to say that we must simply dismiss our cultural presuppositions,
but we do need to identify them and realize that no one culture is
intrinsically better than any another. We also need to be conscious of
the fact that not everyone necessarily sees the world in the same
way. Finally (as we will see in chapter four), the church has declared
that no one culture has "the corner" on the best expression of the
Christian faith. All cultures are capable of expressing the good news
of Christ. At the same time, all cultures are in need of being continu-
ally evangelized—even those that have a long history of contact with
Christianity.

In order to develop an adequate pastoral strategy for dealing
with the challenges posed by the inculturation of the liturgy in the
multicultural context of the United States, we now turn to an
overview of the way the church has dealt with cultural change
throughout history and how these changes have affected the liturgy.

Notes

1. Alfred Kroeber and Clyde Kluckhohn, *Culture: A Critical Review of Concepts and Definitions* (New York: Vintage Books, 1963). Excellent overviews are available that treat the complex relationship of culture and faith from various perspectives. From the point of view of official church teaching, see Hervé Carrier, "Understanding Culture: The Ultimate Challenge of the World Church?" *The Church and Culture since Vatican II*, J. Gremillion, ed. (Notre Dame, Indiana: University of Notre Dame Press, 1985), 13–30. From a missiological perspective, see Aylward Shorter, *Toward a Theology of Inculturation* (Maryknoll, New York: Orbis Books, 1989), 17–30; Gerald

Arbuckle, *Earthing the Gospel: An Inculturation Handbook for the Pastoral Worker* (Maryknoll, New York: Orbis Books, 1990), 26–78. For a more philosophical perspective that takes into account postmodernist and globalizing trends, see Michael Paul Gallagher, *Clashing Symbols: An Introduction to Faith and Culture* (London: Darton, Longman & Todd, 1997), 11–23; Robert J. Schreiter, *The New Catholicity: Theology between the Global and the Local* (Maryknoll, New York: Orbis Books, 1997), 46–61.

2. See Schreiter, *The New Catholicity,* for an insightful treatment of the effects of globalization on inculturation.

3. One need only read University of Chicago professor Allan Bloom's popular *The Closing of the American Mind* (New York: Touchstone Books, 1988) to see that this understanding of Western culture is alive and well in the academy.

4. Bernard Lonergan, *Method in Theology* (London: Dartman, Longman & Todd), 301.

5. See also Stephen Happel's discussion of Lonergan's insight as applied to liturgy, "Classicist Culture and the Nature of Worship," *Heythrop Journal* 21 (1980): 288–302. Because of a lack of attention to matters of normativity, the classicist notion of culture also seems to undergird some of what has been proposed as the "Recatholicization" liturgical movement described by M. Francis Mannion in "Agendas for Liturgical Reform," *America* 175:17 (November 30, 1996): 9–16.

6. Hilaire Belloc, *Europe and the Faith* (New York: Paulist Press, 1920), 261.

7. James J. Walsh, *The Thirteenth, Greatest of Centuries* (New York: Catholic Summer School Press, 1907). This book, lauding the beginning of the medieval universities and "true" Catholic thought, was kept in print well into the 1940s, attesting to its popularity in Catholic circles.

8. Lonergan, 326–27

9. The critique and relativization of Western culture, however, did not originate with the anthropologists of the late nineteenth century. French *philosophes* of the Enlightenment such as Rousseau, in works such as *Émile* (1762), accused Western European social institutions of corrupting rather than educating the young. In a more satiric vein, Voltaire's *Candide* ridiculed Christian pretensions of superiority, especially in religious matters. Among the first and truly empirical observations on culture, though, are those by Charles Seconat, Baron de Montesquieu, who compared the reactions of opera audiences in England, France and Italy. On this, see Shorter's very helpful treatment in his *Toward a Theology,* 20–21.

10. Karl Rahner, "Towards a Fundamental Theological Interpretation of Vatican II," *Theological Studies XIV* (1979), 717.

11. Clifford Geertz, *The Interpretation of Cultures* (New York: Basic Books, 1973), 89.

12. Louis J. Luzbetak, *The Church and Cultures: New Perspectives in Missiological Anthropology* (Maryknoll, New York: Orbis Books, 1996), 165.

The Interplay between Culture and Liturgy throughout History

E xcept for the period of 400 years after the Council of Trent, the history of the liturgy is a story of how Christian worship changed as the church moved into new cultural contexts. This process, of course, is both natural and necessary. Liturgy, as the public worship of the church, celebrates who we are and who we are called to be because of God's love for us in Jesus Christ. Our common worship expresses our identity as God's people, redeemed by Christ's suffering, death and resurrection.

But this proclamation must be done in the context of a given place and time—in a given culture. Religion and culture are intrinsically related—almost like two sides of the same coin. It is for this reason that the theologian Paul Tillich once noted that "religion is the substance of culture and culture is the form of religion."[1] While the message of Jesus Christ transcends culture, it can only be experienced and expressed in a cultural form. For this reason, it is crucial that we in the United States understand the dynamics through which culture has influenced the liturgy over the course of history, lest we confuse its contingent cultural expression with the gospel itself.

In this chapter we will see that inculturation did not occur to the same degree in every place and time. Depending on many circumstances—especially the relationship of the church to the dominant culture—the form of Christian worship was adapted and at times radically transformed to speak to people of new cultures. Since the history of the liturgy is such a vast area of study, we will limit our examination to watershed moments when the worship of the church underwent profound modification due to cultural challenges. We will begin by looking at how culture affected the first Christian communities and their worship.

Inculturation and the First Generation of Believers

Christianity was born in a multicultural world. Space does not permit a detailed analysis of the cultural background of first-century Palestine.[2] However, in order to appreciate how culture affected worship as it developed among the first followers of Christ, it is important to understand that the church's earliest members came from two distinct cultural worlds: a more conservative Judaism, which was Hebrew- and Aramaic-speaking; and a more international, "liberal" Judaism, comprised of predominantly Greek-speaking (Hellenized) Jews. While the Acts of the Apostle is at pains to show the unity of the church (see, for example, Acts 4:32–34), if one reads carefully the pages of the New Testament, it is obvious that there was a division among the first followers of Christ along these same cultural and linguistic lines. Even before the issue of admitting Gentile converts to the new faith was raised, there was the telltale sign of division and discord: Two different groups are identified by name.

> Now during those days, when the disciples were increasing in number, the Hellenists complained against the Hebrews because their widows were being neglected in the daily distribution of food. (Acts 6:1)

21

What was the cause of this neglect? Reading between the lines reveals that the cause is largely cultural. To simplify matters, the "Hebrews" in the passage were those "conservatives" who held that being a follower of Christ was a matter of being a special kind of Jew who recognized Jesus as the Messiah (the Christ). Their language was Hebrew (probably also Aramaic, another Semitic language), and they were faithful to the law of Moses as practiced by other Jews of the time. The other group, the "Hellenists," were also Jews but spoke Greek and were therefore more influenced by the international (Hellenistic) cultural currents of the day. Interestingly enough, one of the key areas of disagreement between the two groups concerned liturgy, specifically the status of the Temple in Jerusalem after the death and resurrection of Jesus Christ. For the Hellenists, whose spokesperson in the early part of the Acts of the Apostles is Stephen, the Temple is no longer necessary; Jesus has replaced the Temple. Significantly, before Stephen is stoned to death, he is accused of both wanting to do away with the Temple and changing Jewish custom (Acts 6:13–14). For the Hebrews, on the other hand, adherence to the law of Moses and to Temple worship was not inconsistent with being a follower of Christ.

The Hebrews and the Hellenists, then, for reasons of both theology and culture, seem to have lived and worshiped a bit differently. The Hebrews not only met in homes for the eucharist and attended Hebrew- or Aramaic-speaking synagogues, they also attended the prayers (and probably sacrificial worship) in the Temple. The Hellenists most likely limited themselves to praying in Greek-speaking synagogues and "breaking bread" (eucharistic sharing) at home. Since the eucharist for both groups was celebrated in the context of a full meal, whether or not the Jewish dietary laws were observed was an important consideration. While we can only speculate, it would seem likely that the Hellenists would have been less rigorous than the Hebrews in interpreting the Mosaic law regarding kosher restrictions (clean and unclean foods) and would have been naturally more open to eating with Gentiles. It is telling that two of the three elements of the decree of the so-called Council of Jerusalem (c. 50 CE), which stipulated the conditions under which Gentiles were to be received into the church, deal with "table manners," that is, dietary restrictions.

> For it has seemed good to the Holy Spirit and to us to impose on you no further burden than these essentials: that you abstain from what has been sacrificed to idols and from blood and from what is strangled and from fornication. If you keep yourselves from these, you will do well. (Acts 15:28–29)

With the destruction of the Jerusalem Temple by the Romans in the year 70 CE and the dispersal of the Christian community of Jerusalem, Christianity began to be interpreted more and more through the lens of the "survivors"—the Hellenists and their Gentile converts. This later group, too, was be forced to change its worship, since, as the first century came to a close, they found themselves increasingly unwelcome in the synagogues of the Diaspora because of their belief in Jesus as the Messiah. During the first several centuries of our era, Christianity was predominantly Greek-speaking and lived in the context of Hellenistic (Greek) culture.

What both cultural segments of the early church had in common was a radical reinterpretation—with Jesus Christ as the interpretive key—of the cultural and symbolic material of Jewish religious practices. Eucharist and baptism, for example, have their roots both in Jewish practice and in Jesus' prophetic challenge to the existing cultural and religious *status quo.*

The emergence in the early church of the eucharist as the central act of worship cannot be fully understood apart from the context of the social and cultural strictures surrounding table fellowship in first-century Palestine. One of the most striking aspects of Jesus' ministry was his willingness to subvert the cultural conventions of his day by sitting down at table with all comers, especially those regarded by his contemporaries as unclean and sinful—tax collectors, prostitutes and those who because of social position were unable to observe fully the law of Moses. Eating with sinners was believed to bring their sinfulness on the "pure one" at the table. But Jesus' table ministry

23

turns this cultural and religious conviction on its head. By eating with all comers he enacts a parable that overturns cultural values in order to proclaim that God is *ho philanthropos*—a lover of humanity. Even the Last Supper, celebrated in its Passover context, is one final example of Jesus eating with sinners, since Jesus is fully aware that those who share in this last meal before his death are all going to betray him. As the scripture scholar Norman Perrin notes,

> [t]he central feature of the message of Jesus is . . . the challenge of the forgiveness of sins and the offer of the possibility of a new kind of relationship with God and with one's fellow. This was symbolized by a table fellowship which celebrated the present joy and anticipated the future consummation; a table fellowship of such joy and gladness that it survived the crucifixion and provided the focal point for the community life of the earliest Christians, and was the most direct link between that community life and the pre-Easter fellowship of Jesus and his disciples.[3]

This reinterpretation of an existing symbol also gave rise to Christian baptism—a ritual washing with water deemed necessary to enter into the community of believers. Variations of this ritual washing with water were widespread in the first century, and there were numerous "baptist movements" in Palestine at the time of Jesus. John the Baptist and his followers were but one example of similar movements that used ritual washing as a sign of penance and conversion to the coming reign of God.[4] The male Essene community at Qumran that produced the Dead Sea Scrolls also prescribed daily ritual bathing as a sign of purification and preparation for the awesome Day of the Lord, when the Messiah would come and vindicate the faithful of Israel.

The Christian practice of baptism was a radical reinterpretation of these existing religions practices that emphasized the meaning of the revelation of God's love poured out on humanity in Christ. Redemption in Christ was soon understood to be open to people who had previously been unclean (such as Gentiles) because "God shows no partiality" (see Acts 10:34–36). As Gordon Lathrop observes,

Christian practice welcomed the cultural symbolism of an eschatological resistance movement: full-body washing to be ready for the day of God. But it rejected repeated washings, self washings, and washing only for men because it reinterpreted the "day of God" to be the presence and gift of the crucified Christ, thereby reinterpreting "purity" to be nearness to Christ, reception of the grace of the Triune God. . . . The resultant washing became the way to enter into Christ's community, his "body," the ragged community which was the reinterpreted "holy people."[5]

The Christian ritual practices of eucharist and baptism did not "fall from the sky," but have their origin in the same Jewish and Hellenistic culture that gave birth to the church. The first believers, in order to be faithful to the memory of Jesus, continued Jesus' radical reinterpretation of Jewish religious and cultural traditions—especially in light of preaching the good news to Gentiles. Many of the liturgical traditions and ritual practices of Judaism were also maintained by the early church, even though these were unfamiliar to Hellenistic culture.[6] Public reading and commentary on the scriptures, the laying on of hands in healing and consecration, and the observance of the beginning of the liturgical day at sundown are all derived directly from Jewish practice and were maintained by the early Christians.

Maintaining the use of words from Hebrew or Aramaic also signaled to native Greek-speakers the fact that the belief in Jesus as the Messiah originated in a culture and language other than their own. While the Hebrew scriptures had been translated into Greek before the first century, it is all the more significant that the early church wished to maintain this contact with Hebrew, especially in the liturgy. This cultural connection with Hebrew and Aramaic remains in our worship to this day. Words like the Hebrew *halleluia* ("God be praised"), *hosanna* (*hoshi-a na;* "Yahweh, save!"), the Aramaic *maranatha* ("come, Lord"), and the Hebrew *amen* ("so be it") were retained by Greek-speaking Christians and are still voiced in worship by most Christians today, regardless of the language they speak.

Christians of the Second and Third Centuries

By the end of the first century, the center of gravity of the new religious movement now known as Christianity had shifted from Jewish Palestine to the Greco-Roman cities of the Roman Empire. This shift not only involved culture and language, it also involved social life. From the villages and small towns of Palestine, where the original "Jesus movement" was born, to the growing urban areas of the Roman Empire, peripatetic preachers like Paul found ready converts to Christianity among people who felt largely indifferent to or disenfranchised from the civic religion of the Greco-Roman city.[7]

What of worship during this period? Undoubtedly, there was a diversity of practices with some constant features.[8] From what we can piece together from the historical evidence, a constant feature was the water-bath administered in the name of the Trinity for forgiveness of sins and entrance into the community of believers. The sacred meal of the Christian community, generally known throughout the Mediterranean region by the Greek word *eucharistia* ("thanksgiving"), was also a constant. It seems that very early on, perhaps soon after Paul wrote to the Corinthians about abuses in their celebration of the Lord's Supper, the eucharist was no longer celebrated in the context of a full meal. As far as the exact details of worship during the first few centuries go, however, we can only surmise that there was a great deal of variation on the local level. The actual words of the liturgy must have depended on the particular skill of the presider, who prayed spontaneously when the church came together.[9] There were no liturgical books other than the treasured copies of the Bible—the Greek version of the Hebrew scriptures and what are described by Justin Martyr around the year 150 as the "memoirs of the Apostles called gospels."[10] The gathering of small numbers of Christians in private homes lent a more informal, familial atmosphere to their worship.

Christian liturgy during this period, like the faith itself, could best be described as countercultural. The most observable traits of the new religion—the ways Christians worshiped—contrasted greatly with the many pagan religions practiced at the time. Most of these religions, both the major civic cults to the Greek and Roman gods and those of the increasingly popular Eastern deities such as Isis and Mithras, practiced animal sacrifice as their principal form of worship. Christian rejected virtually all that was associated with the pagan religious system—priests, temples, altars, animal sacrifices, burning incense to an image of the emperor. As a result, they, in turn, were accused of atheism by their fellow citizens because they rejected these outward signs of Greco-Roman religious practice. Early Christian apologists wrote precisely to refute these charges. One apologist defended Christians by saying that their sacrifice was really the knowledge of the one true God:

> [A]s to our not offering sacrifices: the fashioner and Father of the universe has no need of blood, nor of the savor of fat, nor of the fragrance of flowers and incense. . . . Instead, the best sacrifice to Him is that we know who it was who stretched out the heavens, gathered them into a sphere, and fixed the earth as a center.[11]

Christians not only worshiped differently from others but followed a different standard of conduct. For many of the early Christians, conversion to Christianity entailed a change in their moral life. Candidates for entrance into the catechumenate were obliged to leave professions or trades considered incompatible with the gospel. Professions that required the shedding of blood, such as soldier, gladiator, charioteer, and magistrate (who could impose capital punishment), were forbidden, as were trades associated with pagan-ism and sexual immorality—pagan priest, astrologer, idol-maker, prostitute, unfaithful concubine and brothel-keeper.[12]

In addition, Christians gathered not in temples but in homes, sometimes remodeled to accommodate the growing number of faith-ful. But these house churches usually accommodated a relatively small number of people, only 30 to 50 by some estimates.[13] Edward Foley describes these structures:

> Large homes for the wealthy—usually four-sided structures built
> around a square, open courtyard—were found in virtually every
> urban center of the empire. Their large dining rooms (well suited
> for the eucharist) . . . made them serviceable buildings for Chris-
> tian worship. Structurally, this type of house faced inward with
> rooms that opened into the courtyard at the center of the building.
> The resulting interior provided shelter from the commotion of
> the street and from the disapproving gazes of the pagan neighbors
> and the authorities.[14]

There was, however, a dialogue between the early church and Greco-Roman culture that resulted in liturgical inculturation. Practices that were not intrinsically linked to pagan worship were incorporated into Christian worship and interpreted in light of the scriptures. For example, a document ascribed to a Roman presbyter named Hippolytus known as the *Apostolic Tradition,* which many scholars believe dates from the early part of the third century, reports that the newly baptized were given a mixed drink of milk and honey and a drink of water before receiving the eucharistic wine for the first time. Hippolytus explains the significance of this action as "the fulfillment of the promise God made to the patriarchs, that he would give them a land flowing with milk and honey."[15]

Significantly, this type of drink would have been familiar to a newly-baptized Christian because of its similarity to a family ritual called the *susceptio.* It was already an ancient practice by the first century for a newborn child to be placed on the ground at the feet of the *paterfamilias,* the head of the household. By ancient custom, the *paterfamilias* had the power of life and death over members of the family, and this right was exercised when he decided either to pick up the newborn and thereby acknowledge the child or to simply walk away. If the infant was not believed to be his progeny, or if it was malformed in any way, or even if it was an unwanted female, the *paterfamilias* walked away and the child was taken away by servants to be exposed on a hillside. If the *paterfamilias* bent down and picked up the infant, the child was given a drink of milk and honey as a sign of welcome into the family and to ward off evil spirits.[16]

Clearly, what is at work in the initiatory eucharist of the early church as described in the *Apostolic Tradition* is an example of a method of inculturation known as "creative assimilation."[17] The same welcoming rite practiced by the surrounding culture to welcome a member of the family is given new meaning to illustrate the significance of full initiation into the church, imaged as the "family of God."[18]

It is important to note that inculturation during this period was selective. The church tried to establish a clear distinction between pagan rites and places of worship and those of Christianity. Significantly, there seems to have been more openness to creative assimilation of cultural elements not directly related to pagan religious practice. Emphasis on the domestic nature of Christian life in the house churches, and the "baptism" of social customs such as the *susceptio,* make initiation into the church an entry into a new extended family, with the bishop as a kind of *paterfamilias.* The image of the church as the *familia Dei,* the family of God, continued to be reflected in the liturgical imagination of those who composed prayers for the liturgy even after the house church became a distant memory.

The "Classical" Roman Rite

Christianity was made a legal religion in the year 313 by the emperor Constantine. From that point on, the church's dialogue with the culture of the Roman Empire became more and more intense, and the wall that divided Christian ritual symbols from pagan social and religious symbols began to crumble. Transformed from a persecuted minority sect to the official religion of the imperial family and the empire, Christianity now had to cope with liturgical and pastoral issues it had never dealt with before.

With the burgeoning number of converts to the young church, the smaller, more familial gathering places of the house churches became inadequate for the needs of larger Christian assemblies.

Throughout the empire the architectural form known as the basilica—
the building used as a royal audience hall, law court and market—was
now used expressly for the Christian liturgical assembly. The way
these spaces were arranged echoed their secular use. The apse, or
far end of the building where the emperor or magistrate was sometimes enthroned to hold court, became the place where the bishop
presided from his *cathedra,* or chair, surrounded by his council of
elders (presbyters), or *presbyterium.* Charles Pietri describes the use
of the Lateran Basilica in Rome as a way to make it possible for a
large number of the clergy and people to worship together with their
bishop (the pope), but in a way decidedly different from the small
house church:

> Even more than this direct physical effort of bringing people
> together, the monumentalisation of the liturgical setting changed
> the style of worship. . . . [S]uch a building did mark out a new
> space for the liturgy. It made possible processions, it gave empha-
> sis to particular areas, the royal way with its special lighting and
> the inner naves, while the outermost naves were darker. In the
> transept, near the altar, there was space for seven offertory tables,
> while the apse became the site of the bishop's chair, placed
> facing the people at the east end.[19]

Not surprisingly, this more public liturgy also became more styl-
ized and formal. During this period the best of the spontaneous
prayers voiced by a bishop or presbyter were written down and collected into books in order to save the assembly from what one North
African church synod called "unskilled and wordy" presiders.[20] The
liturgy also began to reflect the new position of the church in relation
to the political and social order, assimilating ceremonial elements
from the imperial court.

Liturgical vesture in both Eastern and Western Christianity still
reflects the formal dress of officials of the late empire. The stole, for
example, was originally the garb of an imperial magistrate of this
period. In fact, it was in this period that ministry within the church was
codified along the lines of the Roman *cursus honorem,* or civil service,
resulting in the development of the seven ecclesiastical orders. Men

were promoted from one order to the next, with the bishop at the top of the pyramid.[21] This structure was supported by an argument that connected Christian priesthood with the Temple priesthood of Israel, and by a Neoplatonic worldview that saw in this hierarchical arrangement a reflection of the very structure of heaven.[22]

The liturgy was still deeply rooted in the scriptures at this time, but the authors of the period began to mine the Hebrew scriptures, seeing in the sacrificial worship of the Temple a *typos,* a foreshadowing, of Christian worship. Thus, deacons were described as "Levites" and presbyters increasingly called "priests." A sacralization of both the persons ministering to the community and the place where the assembly gathered to pray gradually took place. The *place* of the Christian cult became invested with a holiness that was once reserved for the *people* of the assembly. This sacralization marked a change from the period of the house church and brought the triumphant Christianity of the late empire more in line with pagan religious attitudes toward the sacred.[23] It is during this period that the church moved decisively from predominantly domestic images of family and table in its prayers and catechesis to metaphors that referred to Israel's Temple and the political order.[24]

Liturgy was far from uniform during this period. The major urban centers of the empire each developed unique liturgical practices from the fourth to the seventh centuries. In the eastern part of the empire, the areas around Antioch, Alexandria, Byzantium and Armenia became ecclesiastical centers that developed the four original Eastern traditions, from which the 20 Eastern Catholic churches developed.[25] The best-known Eastern tradition is the Byzantine, named after Byzantium, the original name of Constantinople and the capital of the eastern empire. It was the patriarchate of Constantinople that sent missionaries into eastern Europe; their evangelization gave rise to a number of autonomous Eastern Catholic churches. Albanians, Belarusans, Bulgarians, Croatians, Czechs, Greeks, Hungarians, Romanians, Russians, Ruthenians, Slovaks and Ukrainians all developed their own particular ways of being church—with their own liturgies and laws—while at the same time following the Byzantine tradition that had Constantinople as its apostolic center.

But what of the liturgical practice of Rome—the only patriarchate in the West? Significantly, it was during the fourth century that the language of worship of the Roman church was adapted in order to respond to a changed cultural situation. It must be remembered that the Roman church was predominantly Greek-speaking until the third century. It was around the year 370, during the pontificate of Damasus, that Latin, by then the language of the majority of Roman Christians, definitively found its way into the Roman liturgy. At the same time, Saint Jerome made what would become the definitive Latin translation of the Bible from Hebrew and Greek (the Vulgate, which became the Bible of the Middle Ages for the Western church).

While this change was essentially a pastoral one—to enable the faithful to understand what was being prayed—the style of the Latin adopted for Christian worship was similar in many ways to the language employed both in pagan Roman worship and in the imperial court. With the victory of the church over paganism, there was less concern about incorporating elements previously considered pagan into the liturgy. The litany responses *Libera nos, Domine,* and *Te rogamus, audi nos,* both came from the pagan practice of invoking the gods with a series of intercessory acclamations. The manner in which the Roman Canon (Eucharistic Prayer I) addresses God after the Sanctus, *"Te ígitur clementíssime Pater,"* reflects the standard formula for petitions directed to the emperor at court: "To you, most merciful father."[26]

Inculturation during this period extended beyond the verbal elements of the liturgy. A gesture of reverence that is still prescribed today in the Roman liturgy—kissing the altar and the book of the gospels—finds its origin in the pagan custom of venerating the sacred with a kiss. Some aspects of the liturgical year and church architecture would be hard to understand without a knowledge of previous pagan celebrations such as the *dies natalis solis invicti* (the birthday of the unconquered sun). The feast was celebrated at the winter solstice and was reinterpreted by the Christian church as the annual celebration of the birth of Christ, the "sun of righteousness" spoken of by the prophet Malachi. "Orienting" churches, that is building them to face east, also derives from the pagan Greek and Roman practice of turning toward the rising sun when at prayer.[27] These and similar examples illustrate the church's constant (and sometimes unconscious) attempt to adapt its worship to its changed cultural context by reinterpreting the religious, social and political customs of the culture in which it lived.

This era of the "classical" Roman liturgy, which extended from the fourth to the seventh centuries, is a crucial one from the point of view of modern liturgical inculturation. The reforms of the liturgy that took place after Vatican II were very much influenced by the liturgical movement of the early part of the twentieth century, which looked to the patristic and liturgical sources of this period as a kind of blueprint after which to pattern the liturgical renewal of the Roman rite. The great English liturgical historian Edmund Bishop, writing at the beginning of the twentieth century, lists the characteristics of the classical Roman rite as "simplicity, practicality, a great sobriety and self-control, gravity and dignity."[28] These characteristics also describe the Roman culture of the period. One could also add two other characteristics: legalism and a tendency toward abstraction.[29]

We will see that these values have served in subsequent periods of liturgical reform as a kind of yardstick by which such reforms were measured. One need only read article 34 of the Constitution on the Sacred Liturgy, for example, to see that these cultural values played a key role in the liturgical renewal of Vatican II: "The rites should radiate a noble simplicity. They should be short, clear, and free from useless repetition. They should be within the people's powers of comprehension, and normally should not require much explanation."

The Germanization of the Church and the Liturgy

While the western Roman Empire was disintegrating, an amazing effort at evangelization took place to convert the barbarian tribes that had moved into areas formerly controlled by Rome. During this period the liturgy celebrated throughout western Europe continued to be diverse. While the Roman rite held sway in central Italy, other areas of western Europe developed their own liturgical traditions reflecting local cultures. One can easily see in the style of the prayers found in the various non-Roman liturgical books of this period a mirror of the particular national genius of these peoples. In Ireland, where the harp of the honored bard still functions today as a national symbol, it is not surprising that the prayers of the Celtic rite of Ireland and the British Isles excelled in lyrical compositions and hymnody.[30] The thoroughly Romanized province of Spain produced the so-called Mozarabic or Visigothic rite, centered around the cities of Toledo and Braga, which combined a refined Latin erudition with a special concern for orthodoxy, especially in light of the strength of the Arian heresy on the Iberian peninsula.[31] The province of Gaul produced prayers that tended to be wordy, moralizing and emotional, but which liberally incorporated quotations from scripture.[32] Though all of these rites employed Latin in worship, their style is unmistakably different from the more restrained, abstract and legalistic Roman one.

The diversity of rites would eventually give way to the adoption (and at times the imposition) of the Roman rite throughout the West. The see of Rome commanded enormous respect, being the center of pilgrimage to the shrines of the apostles Peter and Paul, and the only patriarchate in the West. Many pilgrims returned home and imitated the liturgical practices they had witnessed at Rome. In Franco-Germanic lands, Pepin (751–68) and his son Charlemagne (768–814) also saw Roman liturgical tradition as a way to achieve political unity in their domain, and so imposed a uniform liturgy.

While the liturgical unification that Charlemagne promoted used the liturgy of the city of Rome as its base, his borrowing of Roman liturgical forms was not wholesale. Under his auspices a supplement was composed and appended to the Roman sacramentary he had received from the pope. These additional texts included the blessing of the Easter candle (our present Exsultet), as well as ordination prayers, blessings, formulas for consecration of churches and for exorcisms—all of which reflect the characteristic Franco-Germanic verbosity and love of scripture. This supplement was eventually incorporated into the sacramentary and was brought back to Rome, where it became, with a few alterations down through the centuries, the basis for the Roman Missal, which remained largely unchanged until the reforms of Vatican II.

Western medieval culture also came to be reflected in the gestures used in the Roman liturgy. A gesture incorporated into the liturgy during this period is practically synonymous with prayer even today—kneeling with hands held together. This gesture derives from the rite of fealty or allegiance performed by a knight to his feudal lord, and was introduced into the ordination rite for priests toward the end of thirteenth century in Rome, having already been practiced for centuries in the northern part of Europe. A knight would kneel before his liege lord with hands placed together; the lord would place his hands around the knight's as a sign of the lord's authority and the knight's respectful submission. Thus, when a priest to be ordained places his hands between the hands of the bishop to promise obedience, he is imitating that feudal gesture of homage given by a vassal to his suzerain. This gesture contrasts with the classical Greco-Roman prayer stance. In the liturgy of the Mediterranean basilicas of the previous centuries the assembly as well as the priest stood with arms open at prayer for most of the liturgical year.[33]

Recent scholarship has also suggested that the move of the Western church into the Germanic north not only brought elements of Greco-Roman culture to the Germanic peoples, it also introduced a Germanic *weltanschauung,* or worldview, into Western Christianity.[34]

Part of this worldview could be termed "runic consciousness," or the belief that the power of a spell or incantation is capable of affecting human life and changing the world. This concern for the magical was a fundamental aspect of the religious outlook of the Germanic peoples.[35] It is fascinating that a ninth-century Germanic version of the gospel called the *Heliand* purposefully chooses not to reveal the "powerful words" used by Jesus to work miracles, lest the newly converted Saxons seek to learn and use them in their own spells. Jesus, described as "the chieftain's son," makes bread and wine holy by the power of his words and then tells his apostles,

> Always continue to do what I am doing at this supper, tell the
> story of it to many men. This body and blood is a thing that
> possesses power: with it you will give honor to your Chieftain.
> It is a holy image: keep it in order to remember Me, so that the
> sons of men will do it after you and preserve it in this world,
> and thus everyone all over this middle world will know what
> I am doing out of love to give honor to the Lord.[36]

The eucharist is described here as a power-filled magic object—a "holy image" that is produced by the runic words. G. Ronald Murphy, an insightful commentator on the *Heliand,* maintains that the objectification of the eucharistic elements into "powerful things" was congenial to German religious sensibilities. He further observes,

> In cross-culturally interpreting the Eucharist in this manner, the
> *Heliand* poet may be one of the first to have participated in the
> shift of sacramental emphasis . . . to the instrumental, or secondary
> causes beloved of Northern Europeans: the water used in
> baptism . . . and, of course, the bread and wine together with
> their accompanying formulae and gestures [perceived and
> presented] as performative spells. . . . The *Heliand* may be an
> instructive instance of the need, among the Saxons at least,
> for the concept of magic in order to come to serious under-
> standing of the "powers" Christians possessed.[37]

Scholars have speculated that this Germanic preoccupation with objectifying the sacred led directly to the eucharistic controversies over the real presence, as well as the later ecclesiastical legitimization of elevating the elements after the institution narrative in order for those present to engage in "ocular communion."[38] It also seems to explain the rise of Corpus Christi devotions among northern Europeans, as well as the popularity of benediction of the blessed sacrament, first in northern European countries and only later in Italy.[39] It is noteworthy that neither of these practices arose in the neighboring Byzantine churches of eastern Europe. This probably should not be surprising given the historic antipathy of the nations of eastern Europe to German culture.

As the Middle Ages progressed, participation in the liturgy diminished in the Western church. There are several reasons for this. The continued use of Latin as the language of the liturgy, and a new sense of sinfulness and unworthiness that discouraged the reception of the eucharist, led to a drastic drop in the number of communicants at Mass. This gradually transformed the celebration of the Mass from an experience of communal prayer to a sacred drama that re-presented the death of Christ. The relocation of the altar to the back wall of the church, and new instructions that directed the priest to say the sacred words in a low voice (or even inaudibly), encouraged an understanding of the Mass as an action of the priest alone.

The growth of popular devotional practices, heretofore incorporated into the liturgy (such as the adoration of the cross on Good Friday), began to develop outside of the official prayer of the church, which was controlled strictly by clerics.[40] Pilgrimages, processions, novenas and the rosary arose as ways lay people could pray in their own language and express the more emotive side of their faith. These devotions can be understood as a spontaneous attempt to inculturate the prayer life of the church, since they were all celebrated in the language of the people and gave expression to religious sentiments and feelings that the official, cleric-led liturgy was unable or unwilling to articulate.

The Missionary Outreach of the Sixteenth and Seventeenth Centuries

The apparent rejection of centuries of liturgical tradition by the Protestant reformers, as well as a concern to maintain doctrinal orthodoxy, led the bishops of the Council of Trent (1545–63) to reaffirm what they regarded as ancient liturgical tradition. The council left to Pope Pius V the twin charges of purging the celebration of the Mass and other sacraments of abuses, and of enforcing liturgical uniformity to maintain ecclesial unity. As a result, the Tridentine reform of the Mass set in stone a late-medieval order of worship that was governed by rubrics and performed by clerics.

The churches built during this period—such as the Jesuit church of the Gèsu in Rome—resemble theaters in which the faithful, like an audience, "attended" the various ceremonies of the church, which were "performed" in an artistic setting designed to inspire feelings of devotion and awe. In the larger towns, full orchestras and choruses performed settings of the Mass by composers such as Bach, Mozart and Beethoven, settings that resemble the style of the best art music of the age. One noted historian accurately described the liturgy in these settings as "church concerts with liturgical accompaniment."[41] During this age of divine-right monarchy, it is not by chance that many churches resembled throne rooms: The great king of heaven, present in the blessed sacrament, held court, enthroned in an ornate tabernacle on the main altar, surrounded by candles, flowers and incense.[42] The liturgy, however, performed by the priest according to strictly-enforced rubrics, remained untouched by the evolving cultural context.

It was during this same period, though, that the church came into sustained contact with non-European cultures. While the liturgy that was brought to non-European lands was essentially that of the medieval, Counter-Reformation and baroque periods, it is instructive to look at two informal attempts at inculturating worship based on a pastoral need for more effective evangelization.

Colonial Latin America

The liturgy that was first brought to the New World by the missionaries of the sixteenth century was essentially that of medieval Spain and not the rigid Tridentine liturgy of the late sixteenth century.[43] This meant that it was far from uniform and amazingly open to local variation—not only those variations brought by the individual missionary from his particular part of Spain, but, as we shall see, open to the indigenous people's religious sensitivities as well. Elements of the old Mozarabic liturgy were carried to the New World and employed in the celebration of the Mass and the marriage rite.[44]

One of the characteristic elements of the Catholicism that developed in the New World was the catechetical ministry of the religious orders (Augustinians, Dominicans and Franciscans) sent to convert the Native Americans. Naturally, conversion was best accomplished through persuasion rather than coercion, and the missionaries employed a variety of creative strategies for proclaiming the gospel. Using illustrated codices or books, the friars sought to overcome the problem of language and root an understanding of Christian doctrine in the hearts of the native peoples. Sometimes these attempts had rather ironic results. One codex contains a pictorial representation of the Trinity with a Franciscan friar as God the Father![45]

Even more important was the brief revival of the patristic-era catechumenate based on the 1523 *Liber sacerdotalis* of the Dominican Alberto Castellani, who was commissioned by Pope Leo X to compile a ritual book able to deal with the influx of adult Muslims being baptized in southern Italy, Sicily and Spain, which had recently come under Christian military control. Creative implementation of these catechumenal rites in the Americas, including the dramatic presentation of the gospel and church teaching, was an attempt to explain the truths of the faith to the native peoples in more accessible ways. For example, in a hymn used in Mexico about the effect and dignity of baptism, the water of the rite is described as "the jade green water of baptism." For the Aztecs and Mayas, jade was considered one of the most precious stones available and was used as sign of divinity.

Later in the hymn, baptism is called the "divine sweat bath," alluding to a penitential practice in the native religion, which was then used to explain the forgiveness and purification from original sin conferred in baptism.[46] This is an example of "dynamic equivalence"—investing religious images and symbols with Christian meaning—and is an age-old method of inculturation that parallels the *Heliand* and the evangelization of ninth-century Germany.

While this sixteenth-century catechumenate lasted for only one generation in Mexico, inculturation through creative assimilation continued for centuries. One of the best examples is the evangelizers' replacement of human sacrifice and sun worship with the veneration of the cross and adoration of the eucharist. The pre-Columbian solar religion of the Aztecs required that human blood be offered to the gods. Atrium crosses in colonial churches in Mexico often resemble Aztec and Mayan iconography, which features cross-like cosmic trees with obsidian mirrors located at the center of the cross. The popularity of these crosses, complete with cosmic symbols and sometimes built on bases representing the altar of holocausts of the Jerusalem Temple, illustrate a "unique conflation of solar imagery and Christ's Eucharistic sacrifice on the cross."[47]

The fashioning of monstrances for eucharistic exposition made to look like sunbursts also seems to have originated in South America. These were used in conjunction with special porches faced with mirrors that were attached to the outside eastern walls of colonial churches in Peru and Bolivia. It seems to have been a widespread practice to expose the blessed sacrament after morning Mass on these mirrored porches in the light of the rising sun. This conflation of eucharistic adoration with sun worship is all the more striking when one considers that many of these churches were built on former sacred sites where the sun was worshiped.[48] This practice was condemned by local church councils at the end of the eighteenth century, but this substitution of eucharistic adoration for human sacrifices to the sun god is a classic example of capturing the religious imagination of people through creative assimilation and substitution.

The Chinese Rites Controversy

Another exception to the Counter-Reformation insistence on liturgical uniformity was an experiment promoted by Matteo Ricci, a Jesuit missionary in China. This experiment became the object of a bitter controversy from 1610 to 1742. Ricci obtained important permissions from the Holy See to adapt the Mass, liturgical vestments and the language of the liturgy to Chinese culture. He also urged that the Chinese practice of honoring their ancestors by bowing before ancestor tablets, derived from Confucianism, not be interpreted as idolatry or superstition, but permitted to Chinese converts by the church. Ricci rightly regarded this custom as an integral part of Chinese identity.

Ricci's attempt at rooting the gospel and the worship of Chinese Catholics in their own culture was met with caustic comments from other missionaries, notably the Dominicans, who accused Ricci and the Jesuits of promoting idolatry. In a very interesting instruction to the Vicars Apostolic of the Far East issued by *Propaganda Fide* in 1659, the idea of transplanting European religious customs to China in order to evangelize was labeled "absurd":

> Do not for any reason of zeal attempt to . . . persuade those people
> to change their rites, customs, and ways unless they are most
> obviously contrary to the Faith and good morals. For what could
> be more absurd that to carry France, Spain, or Italy, or any other
> part of Europe into China? It is not this sort of thing you are to
> bring in but rather the Faith.[49].

The instruction clearly draws a distinction between the faith and its European cultural expression, and states that the faith does not demand that rites and customs of non-Europeans be repudiated or destroyed in order for them to become Christian. Rather, Chinese rites and customs are to be preserved intact in order to serve as vehicles for evangelization, provided they are not "depraved."[50] This instruction, therefore, lays down the principle of liturgical inculturation that later would be echoed by Pius XII[51] and reflected in article 37 of Vatican II's Constitution on the Sacred Liturgy. Unfortunately, the sensitivity of both Matteo Ricci and *Propaganda Fide* were forgotten in the years that followed. Chinese ancestral rites were eventually condemned by Benedict XIV[52]—a move that "spelled the loss of China and Indochina to the church."[53]

A Record of Inculturation

As we have seen, inculturation is almost synonymous with the history of the liturgy. The liturgy has always interacted with local cultures, transforming them and being itself transformed. As the 1994 instruction *Varietates legitimae* (Inculturation and the Roman Liturgy) observes,

> During the course of the centuries the Roman rite has known how to integrate texts, chants, gestures and rites from various sources and to adapt itself in local cultures in mission territories, even if at certain periods a desire for liturgical uniformity has obscured this fact. (#17)

But has this integration always been successful? Depending on the church's relationship with the culture in which it was living, this adaptation was at times superficial and incomplete, and at other times much more profound. From our brief review of history we can safely say that the Roman rite is far from purely Roman but contains elements from a variety of sources, some of which are better integrated than others. Thus, it is easy to concur with David Power when he asserts that

> after the first liturgical transition from Greek to Latin and Roman culture, no full inculturation ever took place when the Roman liturgy was brought to peoples of other cultures. All in all, the hybrid character of European Christianity should tell us that it is possible to have a common book and rubrical unity, but not a liturgical and devotional one. At best the liturgical remains bookish and rubrical, or is augmented by unprescribed devotional practices in order to find a place in the heart of its participants.[54]

It seems that whether consciously or not, human culture will always have an impact on the way Christians worship. The Second Vatican Council, however, was the first ecumenical council of the church that intentionally dealt with the issue of culture and its influence on the liturgical expression of faith. Mindful of the historic interplay between liturgy and culture, we now turn specifically to the documents of Vatican II and to the process that was set in motion by the Council to allow the inculturation of the Roman rite throughout the world.

Notes

1. Paul Tillich, *Theology and Culture* (New York: Oxford University Press, 1959), 42.

2. See the fascinating studies by James Dunn, *Unity and Diversity in the New Testament: An Inquiry into the Character of Earliest Christianity* (London: SCM Press, 1977), and Martin Hengel, *The "Hellenization" of Judaea in the First Century after Christ* (London: SCM Press, 1989). For a more detailed treatment of this theme, synthesizing these and other sources, see my *Liturgy in a Multicultural Community* (Collegeville, Minnesota: The Liturgical Press, 1991), 20–38.

3. Norman Perrin, *Rediscovering the Parables of Jesus* (New York: Harper & Row, 1967), 107. See also Nathan Mitchell's insightful treatment of the countercultural aspect of Jesus' table ministry in *Eucharist as a Sacrament of Initiation* (Chicago: Liturgy Training Publications, 1994), 47–104.

4. See G. R. Beasley-Murray, *Baptism in the New Testament* (London: Macmillan and Co., Ltd., 1962).

5. Gordon W. Lathrop, *Holy People: A Liturgical Ecclesiology* (Minneapolis: Fortress Press, 1999), 181.

6. See an excellent collection of essays on the relationship between Jewish and Christian worship in Eugene Fisher, ed., *The Jewish Roots of Christian Liturgy* (New York: Paulist Press, 1990), and Carmine DiSante, *Jewish Prayer: The Origins of the Christian Liturgy* (New York: Paulist Press, 1991).

7. For a social history of early Christianity see, for example, Wayne A. Meeks, *The First Urban Christians* (New Haven, Connecticut: Yale University Press, 1983). On the religious malaise that facilitated conversion to Christianity, see Thomas Finn, *From Death to Rebirth: Ritual and Conversion in Antiquity* (New York: Paulist Press, 1997).

8. For a highly readable exposition of this period, see Kenneth Stevenson, *The First Rites: Worship in the Early Church* (Collegeville, Minnesota: The Liturgical Press, 1989), and Edward Foley, *From Age to Age* (Chicago: Liturgy Training Publications, 1991), 3–24.

9. Allan Bouley, "Extemporized Eucharistic Prayer in the First Three Centuries," in *From Freedom to Formula: The Evolution of the Eucharistic Prayer from Oral Improvisation to Written Texts* (Washington, D.C.: Catholic University of America Press, 1981), 89–158.

10. *First Apology,* 64.

11. Anthenagoras of Athens, *The Plea;* see also Minucius Felix, *Octavius.* Both are collected in Daniel Sheerin, *The Eucharist.* (Message of the Fathers of the Church 7; Wilmington, Delaware: Michael Glazier, 1986), 28–29, 37–38.

12. Both Tertullian and the *Apostolic Tradition* ascribed to Hippolytus mention this requirement. See Maxwell E. Johnson, *The Rites of Christian Initiation: Their Evolution and Interpretation* (Collegeville, Minnesota: The Liturgical Press, 1999), 79.

13. See Marcel Metzger's description of the house church preserved at Dura Europos in the Euphrates in *History of the Liturgy: The Major Stages* (Collegeville, Minnesota: The Liturgical Press, 1997), 37.

14. Foley, *From Age to Age,* 27.

15. Bernard Botte, ed., *La Tradition Apostolique de Saint Hippolyte,* LQF 39 (Münster: Aschendorfsche Verlagbuchandlung), 21, 56. For an English translation, see G. Cuming, *Hippolytus: A Text for Students* (Grove Liturgical Studies 8; Nottingham: Grove Books, 1976).

16. Pauly-Wissowa, ed., *Real-Encyclopedie der classischen Altertumwissenschaft* (Stoccard: J. B. Metz Buchhandlung, 1932), 30:1570–71. See also Anscar Chupungco, "The Early Cultural Setting of the Baptismal Liturgy," *Tradition and Progress* (Washington, D.C.: The Pastoral Press, 1993), 1–18; Paul Veyne, "From Mother's Womb to Last Will and Testament," in P. Ariès and G. Duby, gen. eds., *A History of Private Life from Pagan Rome to Byzantium* (Cambridge, Massachusetts: Harvard University Press, 1987), 9.

17. On the method of creative assimilation, see Anscar Chupungco, "Liturgy and Inculturation," in A. Chupungco, ed., *Handbook for Liturgical Studies II: Fundamental Liturgy* (Collegeville, Minnesota: The Liturgical Press, 1998), 368–69.

18. As Joseph Jungmann points out, though, vestiges of this custom are found long after it drops out of the liturgy of Holy Saturday. In the tenth-century pontifical of Egbert of York, a blessing is prescribed for the Easter Mass—a blessing of milk and honey after the eucharistic prayer. *The Early Liturgy: To the Time of Gregory the Great* (South Bend, Indiana: University of Notre Dame Press, 1959), 139.

19. Charles Pietri, "Liturgy, Culture and Society: The Example of Rome at the End of the Ancient World (Fourth-Fifth Centuries)," *Concilium* 162 (1983): 40. See also John Baldovin, *The Urban Character of Christian Worship: The Origins, Development and Meaning of Stational Liturgy,* Orientalia Christiana Analecta 228 (Rome: Pont. Institutum Studiorum Orientalium, 1987).

20. The Synod of Hippo (393) in North Africa declared in canon 25 that the prayers of *"homines imperiti et loquaces"* needed to be submitted to *fratres instrutiores* before prayed in public, indicating that the liturgy was becoming less spontaneous and that there was more of a concern for orthodox expression.

21. One only need look at our present ordination prayers for priest and deacon, taken from the *Sacramentarium veronense,* to see this theology applied. On this, see Anscar Chupungco, "Early Cultural Setting of the Ordination Rites," *Sound Tradition and Legitimate Progress* (Washington, D.C.: The Pastoral Press, 1994), 43–65.

22. See this development outlined in G. H. Luttenburger, "The Decline of Presbyteral Collegiality and the Growth of Individualization of the Priesthood (4th to 5th Centuries)," *Recherches de théologie ancienne et médiévale* 48 (1981):14–58; Nathan Mitchell, *Mission and Ministry: History and Theology in the Sacrament of Order* (Wilmington, Delaware: M. Glazier, 1982); and Mary Collins, "The Public Language of Ministry," *The Jurist* 41 (1981): 261–94.

23. J. G. Davies, "The Introduction of the Numinous into the Liturgy: An Historical Note," *Studia Liturgica* 8 (1971–1972): 216–23.

24. This change in describing Christian worship is well illustrated by mystagogical catecheses (post-baptismal instructions to the neophytes) of influential fourth-century Fathers of the church such as Ambrose of Milan, Cyril of Jerusalem and John Chrysostom. See Edward Yarnold, *The Awe-Inspiring Rites of Initiation: The Origin of the R.C.I.A.* (Collegeville, Minnesota: The Liturgical Press, 1994).

25. The 20 Catholic churches following liturgical traditions other than the Latin are the Albanian, Armenian, Belarussian, Bulgarian, Chaldean, Coptic, Ethiopian, Greek, Greek-Melkite, Hungarian, Italo-Albanian, Malabar, Malankar, Maronite, Romanian, Russian, Ruthenian, Slovak, Syrian and Ukrainian; cf. *Annuario Pontificio, per l'anno 1999* (Città del Vaticano: Libreria Editrice Vaticana, 1999), 1158. For an authoritative survey of these churches, their history and relationship to the Orthodox churches, see Ronald Roberson, *The Eastern Catholic Churches: A Brief Survey,* 5th rev. ed. (Rome: Edizioni Orientale Christiana, 1995).

26. Christine Mohrmann, "Quelques observations sur l'évolution stylistique du Canon de la Messe romain," *Études sur le latin des chrétiens III: Latin chrétien et liturgique* (Roma: Edizioni di Storia e Letteratura, 1979): 227–44.

27. On this and other examples see Joseph Jungmann, *The Early Liturgy,* 122–51.

28. Edmund Bishop, "The Genius of the Roman Rite," *Liturgica Historica* (Oxford: Clarendon, 1918), 12.

29. Theodor Klauser, *A Short History of the Western Liturgy* (Oxford: Oxford University Press, 1979), 40–43.

30. Many examples of this are to be found in the *Stowe Missal* (Dublin, Library of the Royal Irish Academy, codex D.II.3; late eighth century), G. F. Warner, ed., Henry Bradshaw Society 31–32 (London, 1906–15).

31. Many of the prayers found in this ancient rite, undergoing a renaissance in Spain at the present time, were composed by the last Western Father of the church, Isidore of Seville, and by his older brother Leandro. See *Liber mozarabicus sacramentorum* (Toledo, Capitular Library, codex 35.3; tenth century), M. Férotin, ed., *Monumenta Ecclesiae Liturgica* 6 (Paris, 1912). A helpful commentary and newly-translated Spanish texts of the Hispanic-Mozarabic rite are found in Antonio Molinero, *Las Otras Liturgias Occidentales* (Bilbao: Ediciones EGA, 1992), 91–126.

32. Of the many extant Gallican sacramentaries, one of the most representative is the *Missale gallicanum vetus* (Rome, Vat. Pal. lat. 493; eighth century), L. C. Mohlberg, et al., eds., (Roma, 1958).

33. On this development see "The Sociological and Religious Significance of Standing and Kneeling" in John K. Leonard and Nathan D. Mitchell, *The Posture of the Assembly during the Eucharistic Prayer* (Chicago: Liturgy Training Publications, 1994), 21–46.

34. See James Russell, *The Germanization of Early Medieval Christianity: A Sociological Approach to Religious Transformation* (New York: Oxford University Press, 1994), and Mary Collins, "Evangelization, Catechesis, and the Beginning of Western Eucharistic Theology," *Louvain Studies* 23 (1998): 124–42.

35. It is this belief that underlies the *Heliand,* an epic poem written in Old Saxon around the year 830, which is a kind of north German version of Tatian's *Diatessaron,* a conflation of the four gospels. See G. Ronald Murphy, *The Heliand: The Saxon Gospel* (New York: Oxford University Press, 1992), and *The Saxon Savior: The Germanic Transformation of the Gospel in the Ninth-Century Heliand* (New York: Oxford University Press, 1989).

36. G. Roland Murphy, *The Heliand,* 153, n. 235.

37. *Ibid.,* 210.

38. For a fine review of this material, see Gary Macy, *The Banquet's Wisdom: A Short History of the Theologies of the Lord's Supper* (New York: Paulist Press, 1992), 67–101.

39. See Mary Collins, "Western Eucharistic Theology," 135–36, where she also notes that Idelfons Herwegen made many of the same general observations of the objectification of the sacred in his groundbreaking book *Antike, Germanentum, Christentum* (Salzburg: Verlag Anton Pustet, 1932), 51–52.

40. On popular religious practice incorporated in the liturgy, see Kenneth Stevenson, *Jerusalem Revisited: The Liturgical Meaning of Holy Week* (Washington, D.C : The Pastoral Press, 1988), 1–12.

41. Joseph Jungmann, "Mass and Baroque Culture," *The Mass of the Roman Rite,* vol. I (Westminster, Maryland: Christian Classics, 1951, 1986), 149.

42. See L. Bouyer's description of the baroque liturgy in *Liturgical Piety* (Notre Dame: University of Notre Dame Press, 1955), 7.

43. Luís Weckmann, *The Medieval Heritage of Mexico,* translated by F. M. López-Morillas (New York: Fordham University Press, 1992), especially 296–312. See also Jaime Lara, "The Liturgical Roots of Hispanic Popular Religiosity," in K. Davis, ed., *Misa, Mesa y Musa: Liturgy in the U.S. Hispanic Church* (Schiller Park, Illinois: World Library Publications), 26–27.

44. Raúl Gómez, Heliodoro Lucatero and Sylvia Sánchez, *Gift and Promise: Customs and Traditions in Hispanic Rites of Marriage* (Hassalo, Oregon: Oregon Catholic Press, 1997).

45. Orlando Espín, "Trinitarian Monotheism and the Birth of Popular Catholicism," *Missiology* 20 (1992): 177–204.

46. Jaime Lara, "Precious Jade Green Water: A Sixteenth-Century Adult Catechumenate in the New World," *Worship* 71 (1997): 427.

47. Jaime Lara, "The Sacramented Sun: Solar Eucharistic Worship in Colonial Latin America," in P. Casarella and R. Gómez, eds., *El Cuerpo de Cristo: The Hispanic Presence in the U.S. Catholic Church* (New York: Crossroad, 1998), 273.

48. *Ibid.,* 278–91.

49. "Instructio vicariorum apostolicorum ad regna synarum tonchini et cocinnae proficiscentium" in *Collectanea Sacrae Congregationis de Propoaganda Fide* 1 (Rome, 1907), 42.

50. *Ibid.*

51. "Summi pontificatus," *Acta Apostolica Sedis* 31 (1939): 429.

52. These rites were condemned by the papal bull *Ex quo singulari* in 1742.

53. Anscar Chupungco, *Cultural Adaptation of the Liturgy* (New York: Paulist Press, 1982), 38. For a detailed history of this fascinating chapter in church history, see George Minamiki, *The Chinese Rites Controversy* (Chicago: Loyola University Press, 1985).

54. David Power, "Inculturation, the Roman Rite, and Plurality of Liturgies," *Pastoral Music* (June–July, 1998), 27.

Chapter Four

The Process of Liturgical Inculturation

Having seen some of the ways the church's worship has changed over the course of history because of changes in culture, we turn now to the decision of the bishops of Vatican II to initiate a process by which the liturgy would sustain a dialogue with local cultures, all the while maintaining what was termed the "substantial unity of the Roman rite." To understand the process, though, we also need to look at how this dialogue matured in the years after the Council. Subsequent experience and further reflection have led to a change in terminology from "adaptation" to "inculturation." This chapter will explore what brought about this change and what effects the change in terminology may have on the process. We will propose four critical relationships between liturgy and culture that must be kept in tension in order to safeguard the authenticity of our worship. These relationships will help us consider several questions. Is the inculturation of the liturgy always and everywhere a positive thing? Can it ever be taken too far? In light of the critical relationships between culture and liturgy, what is involved in the dynamic process of inculturation from the point of view of pastoral ministers?

Vatican II: Culture and Liturgy

When Vatican II convened in 1962, many of the council bishops (and certainly their *periti,* or expert consultants) were aware that the history of the liturgy is a chronicle of the cultural adaptation of worship. Many also had a sensitivity to the Eurocentric self-identification of the church and the need for reorientation as the world's Christian population steadily shifted away from Europe. A record number of participants at the Council were bishops from churches in non-European countries. These pastoral leaders were acutely conscious of the gulf that existed between the celebration of the Mass and sacraments in Latin and the pastoral needs of their people. The presence of bishops from the Eastern Catholic churches and the regular celebrations of their liturgies were constant reminders to the Council fathers that the Roman rite was not the only Catholic way to worship; there are many other liturgical traditions just as venerable and just as orthodox as the Roman.

It is significant that at the beginning of the first document of Vatican II, the Constitution on the Sacred Liturgy *Sacrosanctum concilium* (SC), the Council affirms,

> [I]n faithful obedience to tradition, the sacred council declares
> that the church holds all lawfully recognized rites to be of equal
> legal force and dignity; that it wishes to preserve them in the
> future and to foster them in every way. (#4)

In its Decree on the Catholic Eastern Churches *Orientalium ecclesiarum,* the Council went on to state that the diversity of practice represented by the Eastern churches is part of the heritage of all Christians, thus announcing both the historical and theological precedent for pluriformity within the church, and affirming that unity does not require a stifling and unbending uniformity:

> History, tradition and very many ecclesiastical institutions give
> clear evidence of the great debt owed to the eastern churches by
> the church universal. Therefore this holy council not merely
> praises and appreciates as is due this ecclesiastical and spiritual

heritage, but also insists on viewing it as the heritage of the
whole church of Christ. (#5)

The communion of the Eastern churches in the Catholic church,
each with its particular traditions, theological emphases and liturgical expressions, is an eloquent witness to a cultural diversity within
the one Catholic church. The Council's acknowledgement of this
legitimate diversity ought not to be viewed as a new discovery of the
Council, but a reaffirmation and recovery of what is at heart the
ancient and traditional stance of Christianity to cultural diversity.
Liturgical pluriformity, therefore, is not simply a concession to those
who cannot measure up to Western European norms; it is an intrinsic
aspect of our Catholic heritage and necessary for effective evangelization. As Adrian Hastings has pointed out,

The basic model for cultural diversification of the liturgy should
remain the way worship actually did develop in the early Church.
The Council's very insistence upon the protection of the eastern
rites must necessarily validate the early pluralistic development
of the liturgy out of which both those rites and the Roman rite
emerged. Every rite, including the Roman, is the fruit of a specific
historical inculturation.[1]

Consistent with its statements calling for respecting the traditions
of the Eastern Catholic churches, the Council documents also treat
cultural diversity within the Latin church. While "culture" is occasion-
ally used in a classicist sense, it is clear that the more modern, anthropological understanding of the term undergirds much of the teaching
of Vatican II, especially in its last document, the Pastoral Constitution
on the Church in the Modern World *Gaudium et spes* (GS).[2] Moving
away from an uncritical estimation of Western European civilization
as the superior and normative expression of Christianity, the Council
Fathers speak instead about all people having a "right to culture"
(GS, 60). Because culture, although a human product, is essential to
every person's humanity, to deny or attempt to take away one's culture is clearly unjust. The Council also asserts that the unconscious

(and sometimes conscious) Eurocentrism of the past must give way to a more respectful dialogue with non-European cultures:

> [T]he church has been sent to all ages and nations and, therefore, is not tied exclusively and indissolubly to any race or nation, to any one particular way of life, or to any set of customs, ancient or modern. The church is faithful to its traditions and is at the same time conscious of its universal mission; it can, then, enter into communion with different forms of culture, thereby enriching both itself and the cultures themselves. (GS, 58)

This declaration both relativizes the European cultural expression of the faith and opens the door to a real dialogue with the many cultures in which Christians live. In the years after the Council, the teachings of Pope Paul VI and Pope John Paul II, as well as other official pronouncements of the church's magisterium, continued to develop an understanding of culture and inculturation.[3] Culture is seen as an important vehicle for the development of the person at all levels, including the spiritual. In proclaiming the gospel, the church must take seriously the diversity of human cultures. It follows, then, that it must admit culturally diverse expressions into its liturgies as it did before the Counter-Reformation.

This conviction that there is a need for cultural diversity in the church did not arise in a vacuum. During the first half of the twentieth century, there was an amazing Catholic scholarly renaissance in the fields of scripture, patristics and liturgy. These studies gave the bishops at Vatican II the necessary background and perspective to argue for the validity of cultural pluralism within the church and for the diversity of expression that this pluralism involves. This insight was summed up by a well-known dictum repeated by Pope John XXIII in an encyclical he wrote in 1959: "Let there be unity in what is necessary, freedom in what is doubtful, and charity in everything."[4]

The Constitution on the Sacred Liturgy set Vatican II firmly on the path of allowing local churches a measure of freedom in discovering and developing their own particular expression of the faith in worship. The permission to use the vernacular in the liturgy (see SC,

51

36) and the possibility of legitimate variations within the Roman rite (see SC, 37–40) are examples that might be used to facilitate a better understanding of the liturgy. The principle that the entire liturgy was not set in stone and that it needs to be intelligible to the people who worship is announced early in the document:

> For the liturgy is made up of unchangeable elements divinely instituted, and of elements subject to change. These latter not only may be changed but ought to be changed with the passage of time, if they have suffered from the intrusion of anything out of harmony with the inner nature of the liturgy or have become less suitable. (SC, 21)

It is difficult today to appreciate how revolutionary this statement sounded in 1963. There was at that time a widespread tendency on the part of many Catholics to look upon *all* religious practice— especially the liturgy—as given to the church personally by Jesus, and therefore unchangeable. Most Roman Catholics were unaware of the practices of the Eastern Catholic churches, and it was not unusual for many of the faithful of that era to uncritically assume that the Mass was always celebrated in Latin with the priest's back to the assembly—and that this manner of celebrating the eucharist was what Jesus himself specifically intended. But the Council fathers were aware of the changes that had been made in the rite of Mass over the course of history, and that some of them needed to be corrected.

> [T]he rites are to be simplified, due care being taken to preserve their substance. Duplications made with the passage of time are to be omitted, as are less useful additions. Other parts which were lost through the vicissitudes of history are to be restored according to the ancient tradition of the holy Fathers, as may seem appropriate or necessary. (SC, 50)

It was also clear to the Council bishops that cultural differences affecting how the liturgy is understood had to be taken into account in the process of liturgical renewal. Different cultural contexts may have caused existing liturgical practices to become less "suitable" and therefore among those "elements subject to change."[5] The unbending uniformity in liturgical practice that characterized the

Tridentine rite now gave way to a more pastoral emphasis that allowed the modification of the worship of the local churches in accord with the local culture.

At the same time, however, the renewal of worship mandated by the Council was not to neglect tradition. In fact, it is clear that the basis for the renewal of the liturgy is "sound tradition": "The council also desires that, where necessary, the rites be revised carefully in the light of sound tradition, and that they be given new vigor to meet present-day circumstances and needs" (SC, 4).

What was this "sound tradition"? We saw in the previous chapter that the tradition is extremely rich and quite complex. Article 34 of the Constitution on the Sacred Liturgy gives us an indication by directing that the renewed rites should "radiate a noble simplicity. They should be short, clear, and free from useless repetition. They should be within the people's powers of comprehension, and normally should not require much explanation."

This tradition of "noble simplicity" alludes to the classical Roman rite of the patristic period celebrated in the basilicas of Rome. Many of the major changes in the liturgy promoted by the Council are, in fact, based on the liturgical practices of this period of history: the participation of the assembly in the liturgical action; the freestanding altar with the priest facing the assembly; the full complement of liturgical ministers, such as readers, acolytes and cantors; the proclamation of the word of God in a language all can understand; the elimination of repetitious gestures such as the numerous three-fold signs of the cross and repeated reverences of the altar; and the location of the reserved sacrament away from the body of the church.

While it could be argued that "noble simplicity" is a culture-bound characteristic of the classical Roman rite and not immediately congenial to every culture, the reasons behind the decision to pattern the renewal after the basilican style of worship are both theological and practical. First, there was a concern to be faithful to tradition. The conciliar renewal of the liturgy did not seek to break with the heritage of the West but looked to a period in the history of the

Roman rite when the members of the assembly participated in the liturgy and were not simply in attendance as mute spectators. The period of the classical Roman rite offered a traditional and helpful framework. Second, there was the matter of practicality: It would be easier to adapt a relatively simple order of worship to present-day circumstances than it would be to work with a more complex one. The Tridentine Mass, with its complicated rubrics, was simply not a helpful starting point for the adaptation the Council desired.

The Process of Cultural Adaptation of the Liturgy

A careful reading of the Constitution on the Sacred Liturgy shows that the Council regarded the process of cultural adaptation of the liturgy as essentially a matter of the translation and interpretation into various cultures of the revised standard editions *(editiones typicae)* of the liturgical books.[6] Since these books serve as the starting point for the work of inculturation, it is helpful to be familiar with how these books came to be.[7]

During the 1960s special commissions were established under the auspices of the Congregation for Divine Worship in Rome that were responsible the revision of the liturgy. Over the course of ten years, these commissions—composed of scholars, pastors and other experts in the liturgy, and advised by bishops—revised the liturgical library of the church. Working with the critical sources on the Roman liturgy—the ancient sacramentaries, ordinals, pontificals and rituals—and conscious of the pastoral needs throughout the world, they sought to fulfill the mandate given to them by the Council in article 25 of the liturgy constitution: "The liturgical books are to be revised as soon as possible. Experts are to be employed on this task, and bishops from various parts of the world are to be consulted." The revisions were to be done in light of the overarching concern of the Council for liturgical renewal: full, active and conscious participation in the liturgical celebrations (see SC, 14).

> In this renewal, both texts and rites should be ordered so as to express more clearly the holy things which they signify. The Christian people, as far as is possible, should be able to understand them easily and take part in them in a celebration which is full, active and the community's own. (SC, 21)

The Council proposed a prudent method to be followed in proposing the revised rites.

> [A] careful investigation—theological, historical, and pastoral—should always, first of all, be made into each section of the liturgy which is to be revised. Furthermore the general laws governing the structure and meaning of the liturgy must be taken into account, as well as the experience derived from recent liturgical reforms and from the concessions granted in various places. Finally, there must be no innovations unless the good of the church genuinely and certainly requires them, and care must be taken that any new forms adopted should in some way grow organically from forms already existing. (SC, 23)

Once drawn up, the revised Latin liturgical books were subject to the approval of the pope and the Congregation for Divine Worship. After approval by the Holy See, they became the *editiones typicae,* the standard or "typical" editions of the liturgical books, and were sent to the various national episcopal conferences to be translated into the vernacular of each country. These translations, with any adaptations, were then submitted to the Holy See for its confirmation and subsequently became the official Roman Catholic liturgical books of the local churches.

While it may appear that this process would have produced a rather internally consistent and homogeneous product, the result is a bit more complicated. The most complex liturgical book—owing to its history of revisions, of course—was the sacramentary *(Missale romanum).* The Tridentine missal was a patchwork of texts—some not even Roman—from many periods of history.[8] There was an ancient stratum made up of Roman prayers such as the Roman Canon and traditional Mass formularies like those for Christmas. But the Missal of Pius V also contained compositions from other periods and cultures: the Exsultet from the Gallican church; formularies for feasts of the Lord such as Corpus Christi, which were added during the Middle Ages; and formularies that were added even later, as in the case of those for the Sacred Heart and Christ the King.

In order to fulfill the mandate of the Council to simplify the rites, the commissions not only culled many of the medieval texts that were of lower quality, they also added new material because of pastoral need. Some examples are the solemn blessings at the end of the present sacramentary, which are not Roman but Mozarabic in inspiration. This is also seen in the three additional eucharistic prayers proposed in the sacramentary. These prayers are not even Roman in structure: Eucharistic Prayer II is from the third-century *Apostolic Tradition* ascribed to Hippolytus; Eucharistic Prayer III is a new composition meant to highlight themes from the Roman Canon but organized in what scholars call an Antiochene structure (named after the ancient city of Antioch in Syria); Eucharistic Prayer IV is a modified text of the Anaphora of Saint Basil, and is likewise structured differently from the Roman Canon.[9] If this all seems complicated, that's because it is. The point is that the present sacramentary, even the Latin *editio typica* directly issued by Rome, is a hybrid document that could never be described as purely Roman either in content or style. The *editio typica* itself, before any translation, demonstrates that the Roman rite is a rite influenced by a variety of cultures.

What, then, are we to make of the concern of the Council for "the substantial unity of the Roman Rite"?

> Provided that the substantial unity of the Roman rite is preserved, provision shall be made, when revising the liturgical books, for legitimate variations and adaptations to different groups, regions and peoples, especially in mission countries. This should be borne in mind when drawing up the rites and rubrics. (SC, 38)

It is apparent from the original process of the reform that the substantial unity of the rite cannot be found in "cultural purity" or even in homogeneity in the *editiones typicae*. Rather, as the 1994 instruction *Varietates legitimae* (Inculturation and the Roman Liturgy) indicates, this substantial unity is expressed "in the typical editions of the liturgical books published by authority of the supreme pontiff and in the liturgical books approved by the episcopal conferences for their areas and confirmed by the Apostolic See" (#36).

As the renewal progressed in the 1970s and '80s, national episcopal conferences prepared liturgical books in the vernacular that were based on the typical editions. Understandably, these books differ from one another in presentation and content. For example, the Italian sacramentary has new prayers for Sundays that reflect the three-year cycle of lectionary readings. The rite of funerals prepared by the International Commission on English in the Liturgy, approved by the English-speaking bishops' conferences and confirmed by the Holy See, also contains new prayers for pastoral circumstances that were not addressed in the Roman typical edition.[10]

It is apparent, then, that the "substantial unity" of the rite is not found in a slavish adherence to certain formal characteristics of the Roman style of prayer, or limited to the texts and rubrics of the *editiones typicae*. In fact, a feature of the reformed liturgical books is the discretion given to the presider to offer introductions to various parts of the liturgy in order to promote the active participation of the members of the assembly. While the liturgical books produced after Vatican II are the heirs of the Tridentine books they replace, clearly they are of another, less restrictive variety. Vatican II did not simply swap one set of rigid rubrics and invariable texts for another, and it is a mistake to think otherwise.

It would also be a mistake to think that all the modifications and enrichments made to the typical editions of the liturgical books are of the same order. There is a tendency to use the term "inculturation" to mean anything and everything done at the liturgy with a reference to culture. For example, "inculturation" is commonly used to describe something as superficial as throwing a *serape* on the altar at a liturgy where the assembly is predominantly Hispanic, and something as profound as the composition of new eucharistic prayers that draw on the imagery and rhetoric of a local culture. Clearly it would be helpful to distinguish between superficial and profound levels of inculturation. A look at the origin of the word, and how it came to replace "adaptation," will help us see that inculturation is but one step in the process of the cultural adaptation of the liturgy.[11]

From Adaptation to Liturgical Inculturation

While the use of the term "inculturation" has become common, especially in Catholic circles, it was not part of the vocabulary of Vatican II. The Constitution on the Sacred Liturgy never used the term. Instead, the key articles dealing with culture and the liturgy, "Norms for Adapting the Liturgy to the Temperament and Traditions of Peoples" (SC, 37–40), as well as subsequent articles dealing with the sacraments and sacramentals, use the term "adaptation" *(aptatio, accommodatio)* to speak of how the rites are to be changed to enable them communicate the gospel more effectively to those who celebrate them.[12] Gradually, however, the term "inculturation" became the usual shorthand way to refer to this process.

Inculturation is a neologism that first appeared in the 1960s in an article by the French theologian J. Masson, who called for "a Catholicism that is *inculturated* in a pluriform manner."[13] The term subsequently became popular in theological and missiological circles, and was used in contrast to the anthropological term enculturation, which describes the "cultural learning process of the individual, by which a person is inserted into his or her culture."[14] Related words such as indigenization, incarnation, contextualization, revision, accommodation and acculturation have also entered the theological lexicon to describe the process of more effectively proclaiming the faith in diverse cultural contexts.[15] "Inculturation" became part of the official vocabulary of the church when it was used in 1979 by Pope John Paul II. In an address to the Pontifical Biblical Commission, the Pope admitted that the term was a neologism, but that it "expresses one of the elements of the great mystery of the incarnation."[16]

Why the gradual change in terminology? In the years after Council, concern was raised that "adaptation" was too superficial a term to speak of the profound transformation that is to be brought about by the dialogue between faith and culture.[17] Pope Paul VI clearly stated that the goal of inculturation is a more profound change, since it begins from the perspective of the *hearers* of the gospel—the "people in the pews." In his 1975 encyclical *Evangelii nuntiandi*—probably the best treatment to date in a church document of the relationship between faith and culture—he writes of the importance of going beyond the superficial aspects of a people's way of life and taking their culture seriously as a crucial factor in evangelization:

> [W]hat matters is to evangelize human culture and cultures (not in a purely decorative way, as it were, by applying a thin veneer, but in a vital way, in depth and right to their very roots) . . . always taking the person as one's starting-point and always coming back to the relationships of people among themselves and with God. (#20)

Pope John Paul II, developing earlier church teaching, described inculturation using the analogy of Christ's incarnation.[18] Just as Jesus Christ, the Word of God, became a Jew of first-century Palestine and so was immersed in the Jewish culture of the time, so the church must become incarnated in every culture, speaking that culture's language and using its symbols to communicate the faith. Inculturation is not a process that is secondary to the faith or an option to be implemented depending on circumstances. Rather, adequate cultural expression is a necessary part of how the faith itself is communicated.

> The synthesis between culture and faith is not just a demand of culture, but also of faith. A faith which does not become culture is a faith which has not been fully received, not thoroughly thought through, not fully lived out.[19]

Inculturation in a general sense can best be described as a dialogue between faith and culture that transforms and enriches *both* the culture in which the faith is proclaimed and the universal

59

church.[20] Just as individual cultures are enriched by the gospel, so the church is enriched by yet another way of seeing the grace of God expressed by another culture.[21] As we noted above, and as recognized by Vatican II, the diversity represented by the communion in the one Catholic church of the Eastern Catholic churches and the Roman Catholic church is an example of such enrichment.

Inculturation also implies the conversion and the transformation of both the receiving culture and the church. There are no cultures that are perfectly evangelized. Every culture is called to a more perfect conversion to the gospel. True inculturation entails conversion, a purification of those attitudes and practices in a given culture that do not conform to the gospel of Jesus. Inculturation also involves the humble assessment on the part of the church of the limited way it has sometimes proclaimed the gospel. It is in this dynamic relationship between faith and culture that the transformation brought about by inculturation takes place.

Acculturation

The meaning of inculturation becomes clearer when we study it in light of a related concept—acculturation. Acculturation can be defined as "culture contact," when two cultures come together and produce a juxtaposition of elements that remain unrelated to one another, not really influencing each other. Liturgical acculturation is perhaps best illustrated by a story.

An acquaintance of mine once took a Christmas vacation to Sicily as a seminarian in the 1950s. He and several of his friends went to the cathedral in a major city of the island. They arrived an hour before midnight to a packed church. At the stroke of midnight a formal procession that included acolytes with incense, a processional cross, and a good number of assisting priests (dressed in those days as deacons and subdeacons) began, accompanied by trumpets and organ. Finally, the archbishop entered, not with a crosier or pastoral staff, but carrying a statue of the baby Jesus. As the archbishop entered the cathedral, people stood on their chairs, applauding and whistling. Everyone present was wildly and noisily celebrating the birth of Christ, as was the custom. The archbishop processed up to the front of the church to the crèche located to the right of the sanctuary and placed the statue of Jesus in the manger to more applause and shouts of joy. He then began the Mass—and everyone but the clerics left for home.

This tradition of laying a statue of the baby Jesus in the manger on Christmas Eve, obviously dear to the Sicilians, had nothing to do with the celebration of the eucharist that followed—at least in the minds of the majority of the people, who left after this rite was completed. This is an example of acculturation; the procession with the statue and the eucharistic liturgy were merely placed alongside one another, without any meaningful integration. Acculturation is not a bad thing in and of itself. While not the ideal, it was practically the only way people could express deeply-held cultural values during the baroque period, when the Mass was protected by an impenetrable wall of rubrics. That being said, it nonetheless falls short of the transformation of both culture and church presumed by the term "inculturation."[22]

Translation: Formal Correspondence versus Dynamic Equivalence

The meaning of inculturation can also be illustrated by a reference to the translation of texts. Those who are familiar with more than one language know that translation always requires a degree of interpretation. There is an old Italian play on words that applies here: *traduttore/traditore* (translator/traitor). We sometimes say in English that something "was lost in the translation." This means that not everything expressed in the genius of one language can be translated into another, since syntax and literary convention often contain nuances that are simply not translatable.

A merely acculturated approach to translation would insist on a word-for-word correspondence with the original language. According to this line of thought, fidelity to the original text is rendered only when there is a correspondence in the receptor language of every element in the original text. Due to the legitimate desire to communicate doctrinal nuances and to hand on the faith of the church intact, there are some who believe that formal correspondence is the only acceptable criterion for translation.

The problem with formal correspondence and liturgical translation can be highlighted by offering an example from poetry. When translating a poem, the meaning of the words is important, but the words themselves were chosen by the poet for the effect they have when read aloud. The literal translation into English of the first verse of a famous French poem by Paul Verlaine (1844–96) illustrates the issue:

Les sanglots longs	The long sobs
Des violons	Of the violins
De l'automne	Of autumn
Blessent mon coeur	Wound my heart
D'une langueur	With a monotonous
Monotone.[23]	Languor.

The poet chose long "o" sounds to convey, along with the words, an idea of sobbing and sadness—and monotony. The translation conveys the literal meaning of the words, but because the sounds of the English words are different from the French, the composition no longer sounds the same and the artistry of the poem is lost. In fact, it is likely that Verlaine chose some of the words of the poem not for their meaning but for their sound. The word "violin," for example, was chosen probably because of its two long "o" sounds and not because of the musical qualities of the instrument!

Latin liturgical compositions from the late classical period, although not exactly poetry, also possess a rhetorical form that is lost in English. An important aspect of these prayers is known as *cursus,* or rhythmic prose, a rhetorical element that dates back to ancient

Greece and Rome. Neither prose nor poetry, *cursus* requires the clauses of sentences to close with words chosen to follow certain preordained rules based on accent and syllabification. The ancient Latin prayers of the sacramentary reflect this style, and, much like the sound pattern of the Verlaine poem above, the *cursus* must be considered when translating, since some words could have been used not because of their meaning but because they fill out a desired rhythmic pattern.

A translator unaware of this element in Latin prayers could inadvertently emphasize a word that is present more for the sake of the *cursus* than for the meaning of the text.[24] For example, a word that appears quite often in the petition of presidential prayers is *quaesumus* ("we beseech"). The word itself is not that important since it is often placed in a phrase with another verb of petition simply to lengthen the number of syllables in the line. To emphasize *quaesumus* in translating the petition would be a mistake since it is often present solely for stylistic reasons.[25]

Finally, an acculturated—rather than inculturated—translation is produced when a word is rendered without knowledge of its cultural references. This risks making the text unintelligible. A simple example illustrates this point. In Eucharistic Prayer I (the Roman Canon) we pray that "those who sleep in Christ may find in God's presence light, happiness and peace." The Latin phrase translated by this line is *"locum refrigerii, lucis, et pacis,"* literally, a place "of *refrigerium,*" light and peace. What on earth could that mean? To the ancient Romans the *refrigerium* was the place of refreshment where their blessed dead went after death. It was, as its name implies, someplace cool. (Anyone who has spent the summer in Rome without air conditioning can appreciate this image.) Early Christians retained reference to the *refrigerium* but used it to describe the place where the dead await the last judgement in the presence of God.[26] Clearly, to propose the term *refrigerium* in the translation would make absolutely no sense to English-speaking worshipers, who would only think of refrigerators! The use of "happiness" to translate *refrigerium* more accurately conveys the original sense of the word to the English-speaking hearer. As the Consilium's 1969 instruction on the translation of liturgical texts *Comme le prévoit* rightly insists, "In the case of liturgical communication it is necessary to take into account not only the message to be conveyed, but also the speaker, the audience, and the style" (#6).[27] The same article of the document sums up the task of translation with the criterion of dynamic equivalence, that is, of translation as inculturation:

> [I]t is not sufficient that a liturgical translation merely reproduce the expressions and ideas of the original text. Rather it must faithfully communicate to a given people, and in their own language, that which the Church by means of this given text originally intended to communicate to another people in another time. A faithful translation, therefore, cannot be judged on the basis of individual words: the total context of this specific act of communication must be kept in mind, as well as the literary form proper to the respective language.[28]

Liturgical Inculturation

While it may flow from acculturation and at times overlap it, inculturation is a more profound interaction between the local culture and the liturgy, to the point that the liturgy begins to appear not as an importation but as a reflection of the local culture, which at the same time challenges the culture to conversion. Liturgical inculturation is necessary when elements of the Roman rite are not capable of speaking meaningfully to the people of a given culture without profound modification.

The best-known example of inculturation in our own day may be the so-called "Zairian rite" (the Roman rite for the dioceses of Zaire) approved by the Congregation for the Sacraments and Divine Worship in 1987, following almost 20 years of study and experimentation by the bishops of Zaire. While the principal elements of the Mass are recognizable (as the title indicates, it is the *Roman* rite for the dioceses of Zaire), these elements are celebrated in a context that uses African idioms to explain their meaning. The use of African images in the prayers of the Mass, dance by the liturgical ministers, a reordering of the elements of the ritual (the placement of the exchange of peace after the penitential rite, for example), all combine to give the Roman rite an African expression.[29] Because of the introduction of elements that are completely new to the Roman rite—for example, the addition of the ministry of *annonciateur,* or announcer, who precedes the arrival of the presider and prepares his welcome by the assembly—one could also say that this rite is an example of the most radical level of cultural adaptation, that of creativity.

Creativity

In places where the culture of the local church is greatly different than that presupposed by the Roman rite, liturgical creativity will be necessary for the liturgy to speak to the people of the local culture. In his classic work on inculturation, Robert Schreiter poses several dilemmas confronted by missionaries who have worked in non-Western cultures:

> For example, questions about the eucharistic elements: How is one to celebrate the eucharist in countries where Muslim theocracies forbade the production or importation of fermented beverages? What was one to do in those cultures where cereal products such as bread were not known, in which the uncon-secrated bread itself became a magical object because of its foreignness? Or how was one to celebrate baptism among the Masai in east Africa, where to pour water on the head of a woman was to curse her with infertility?[30]

Provision for "more radical adaptation of the liturgy" is made in the liturgy constitution (SC, 40), which stipulates a process of study and experimentation by the national conference of bishops and then submission of the adaptations to Rome for confirmation. While the need for liturgical creativity in non-Western cultures is obvious, could there also be reason for liturgical creativity in cultures that would be described as predominantly Western European, such as the

United States or Australia? In fact, the 1969 instruction *Comme le prévoit* deals with this possibility for Western cultures as well: "Texts translated from another language are clearly not sufficient for the celebration of a fully renewed liturgy. The creation of new texts will be necessary" (#43). This principle also extends beyond the composition of new texts to the development of new rituals for the celebration of the sacraments and other rites. As Anscar Chupungco points out,

> [T]he rites of marriage and funerals, even if they have been inculturated on the basis of the Roman liturgy, can prove to be culturally inadequate. That is why the Constitution on the Sacred Liturgy 77 has given to the Conference of Bishops the option to draw up a completely new rite of marriage in accord with the usages of place and people.[31]

Whatever is proposed, however, whether new texts or new rites or elements of rites, care needs to be taken that they do not "fall from the sky." Any new text or rite needs to be related in some way to the existing official version of the liturgical books. This follows the principle of "organic progression" enunciated in article 23 of the liturgy constitution: "Care must be taken that any new forms adopted should in some way grow organically from forms already existing."

As we have seen, then, under the umbrella label "cultural adaptation of the liturgy" are three degrees: acculturation, the simple juxtaposition of local cultural elements; inculturation, a reinterpretation (dynamic translation) of Roman liturgical elements in order to communicate more effectively and faithfully the message of the gospel; and creativity, the creation of completely new ritual elements. Acts of inculturation and creativity, of course, require a deep knowledge of the culture of the local church, as well as confirmation of the Holy See. These levels of cultural adaptation were provided for in articles 37–40 of the liturgy constitution, and were further refined in subsequent documents such as *Comme le prévoit* and the 1994 instruction *Varietates legitimae* (Inculturation and the Roman Liturgy).

Four Critical Relationships between Liturgy and Culture

Cultural adaptation of the liturgy is a natural process that has occurred spontaneously in local churches and is now understood as a way of ongoing renewal provided for in the Constitution on the Sacred Liturgy. Because of the new understanding of the importance of all human culture, we know that every time we gather to celebrate the liturgy, culture affects our interpretation of the rites. The rites themselves are complex cultural products, like a palimpsest—a parchment that has been written on several times and bears the marks of different authors. Hebrew, Aramaic, Greek, Roman, Franco-Germanic, medieval and baroque textual and liturgical elements are all present in the rite of Mass. We are not always conscious of the origin of these various elements, but we take them and interpret them in the context of our own U.S. culture. But there still exists the need for criteria against which to judge whether or not our cultural adaptations are faithful to the gospel.

One of the groundbreaking works of this century that explored the relationship between culture and the Christian faith is H. Richard Niebuhr's *Christ and Culture.* Niebuhr distinguishes and describes five typologies or models of the relationship between Christ and culture: Christ against culture, Christ of culture, Christ above culture, Christ and culture in paradox, and Christ the transformer of culture.[32] Some of these typologies are more easily applied to the liturgy than others, and they have been the subject of further reflection by Protestant and Catholic theologians since the publication of the book in 1951.[33] This "models approach" has been found very helpful in efforts to keep different aspects of the relationship between faith and culture simultaneously before our eyes, since the relationship itself is dynamic, fluid, and at heart paradoxical.

The work done by an ecumenical consultation on culture and liturgy of the Lutheran World Federation builds on and refines the models approach to liturgy and culture. At a 1996 meeting held in

Nairobi, Kenya, the working group helpfully distinguished at least four different ways in which a received liturgical tradition (in our case, the Roman rite) relates dynamically to local culture: transculturally, contextually, counterculturally and cross-culturally.[34]

The Roman rite relates *transculturally* to local cultures in that there are elements in the rite that "are not subject to change" and will be invariable in all cultures and in all places. Examples of these elements include gathering in the name of Christ, reading from the scriptures, a prayer of praise and thanksgiving to the Father through the Son in the Spirit over the eucharistic elements, sharing in the eucharist, and baptism in water in the name of the Trinity.

Our liturgy also relates *contextually* to culture. This refers to the process of the cultural adaptation of the liturgy. Through acculturation, inculturation and creativity, the church's worship is modified and transformed to make the message of the gospel expressed in the rite more understandable and compelling. The dynamic translation of the prayers and other texts from the *editio typica,* as well as the introduction of cultural elements that enrich the celebration in a given culture, are two ways that the liturgy is contextualized or inculturated. The overarching criterion for these changes is their faithfulness to the gospel and their "organic relationship" to the liturgical tradition.

A third way in which our received liturgical tradition relates to culture is *counterculturally.* No culture is free of the effects of human sinfulness. There are elements in every society that are dehumanizing and contrary to the good news we have received in Jesus Christ. Unjust divisions between rich and poor, oppression of the defenseless, unbridled materialism and selfish individualism all need to be challenged by the liturgy because they are contrary to the will of God expressed in the gospel. Our liturgical celebrations must give witness to this truth and give voice to the call to holiness that we have received from God. As the late liturgist Mark Searle used to say, our liturgical celebrations ought to be a kind of rehearsal of the reign of God announced by Jesus.

One of the scriptural images of this reign is of a lavish meal at which all are invited. At this feast all God's people experience equality, peace and joy in the Holy Spirit. It is a dinner party where "business as usual" comes to a halt. At this table, where God's children are gathered, all human attitudes that separate us from one another are forever banned: greed, lust for power and domination, discrimination against the weak and marginalized. Each time we come together at our eucharistic feast, then, we implicitly critique our sinful present reality and pledge to cooperate with God and with one another to bring about God's reign.

The Pontifical Council for Culture recently made this point when it wrote about the transforming power of the gospel on human culture, a power that must be expressed in culturally-rooted ways:

> For the Church, evangelizing means bringing the Good News into all the strata of humanity, and through its influence transforming humanity from within and making it new. . . . The Gospel, and therefore evangelization, are certainly not identical with culture, and they are independent in regard to all cultures. Nevertheless, the kingdom which the gospel proclaims is lived by human beings who are profoundly linked to a culture, and the building up of the kingdom cannot avoid borrowing elements of human culture or cultures. (*Towards a Pastoral Approach to Culture*, 4)

Finally, the fourth way in which the liturgical tradition relates to culture is *cross-culturally*. Just as the Roman rite bears the traces of many cultures (Jewish, Greco-Roman, Franco-Germanic), so it continues to embrace new cultural elements from throughout the world, which in turn are shared by the whole church. Legitimate local variations can be studied and shared among the local churches, thus enriching the universal church. For example, particular musical forms, processional movement and iconography developed through one culture's interaction with the gospel can enrich and inspire the liturgical forms of other local churches. This, of course, is the result of the dialogical dynamic of inculturation which, as John Paul II has stated, both incarnates the gospel in different cultures and at the same time introduces "peoples together with their cultures" into the community of the church.[35]

These four ways that a liturgical tradition relates to culture— transculturally, contextually, counterculturally and cross-culturally— complement one another and must be kept in tension in order to evaluate the ongoing process of inculturation. For example, if we try to inculturate the liturgy inappropriately, not mindful enough of the demands of the gospel, we run the risk of proclaiming a truncated gospel that celebrates our prejudice and sinfulness. A classic example of this was a request made to the Holy See by several German bishops in the 1930s to remove the names of the Jewish matriarchs from the nuptial blessing, since these references were disfavored by the Nazis. Given the anti-Semitic context of Germany in the 1930s, this "adaptation" of the marriage rite would have been very popular among Germans seeking to ingratiate themselves with the Nazis. To its credit, the Holy See rejected this request out of hand.[36] On the opposite end of the spectrum, a refusal to change and adapt to culture, or to deny that our liturgical tradition can learn from other cultural expressions of the faith, is equally problematic.

The Pastoral Context

It is helpful to see that the relationship between faith and its liturgical expression depends on various elements within the pastoral context. This context can be envisioned as a circle with four parts that are in constant interaction. These parts are the gospel as it is expressed in the liturgical tradition; the pastoral agents, who interpret the tradition and make decisions regarding the community's worship; the cultural context of the local assembly; and the social change that attends every culture.[37] These four elements need to be kept in constant dialogue in order for our attempts at liturgical inculturation to be both responsible to the tradition and sensitive to the assembly's cultural setting.

We are all profoundly affected by our culture. This is true not only of individual ministers but of every human being—even the members of the Congregation for Divine Worship in Rome! We need to acknowledge that our personal *en*culturation affects the decisions we make concerning liturgical *in*culturation. It is also here that our own theology, spirituality and psychology will influence how we perceive the relationship of liturgy to the surrounding culture. For example, if the only people who have a say in the decisions that affect the community's worship are white, middle-class, male and celibate, then the unique insights of whole sectors of the parish will not be expressed, and the liturgy will be impoverished because of it. This can also be true for pastoral agents who minister in a culture other than their own. Familiarity with a culture—even living in that culture for a long period of time—does not guarantee that one truly understands that culture and the nuances of its signs and symbols.

A key characteristic of those who are able to carry out successfully the ministry of inculturation is a willingness to listen and learn from the people to whom they minister. Knowledge of the liturgical tradition and "the norms governing the valid and lawful celebration" of the liturgy are not sufficient.[38] Ministers that want to facilitate responsible inculturation also need to see the cultural context of their ministry as a potential source of the revelation of God's grace. They must be willing to take the time to learn from the surrounding culture. Peter Schineller describes the ministry of inculturation this way:

> The ministry of inculturation means serving, putting the needs of
> the situation before one's own agenda. The agent of inculturation
> enters the situation with respect and humility, knowing that
> he or she treads on holy ground and at the invitation of those
> concerned. He or she comes with the conviction that God is
> already present in the situation.[39]

What Schineller describes here is not simply a pastoral technique, but a ministerial spirituality that touches at the heart of the task of inculturation. He then sketches the attitudes of ministers who are sensitive to inculturation:

Among the many attitudes or dispositions needed by the agent of inculturation are the following. One must be patient, since the acceptance of the gospel values depends on human freedom and the grace of God. . . . At the same time that one ministers as an agent of inculturation, one must let oneself be ministered to. And in addition to offering resources as a teacher, one must be willing to learn. It is this last point that makes the process of inculturation so exciting, for in the process of sharing and giving, one receives some portion of the hundredfold. One's own faith is deepened and one's vision broadened. Above all one needs a listening heart—an ability to listen to the call of God as it comes through the tradition, and, equally important, an ability to listen to the call of God as it comes through the persons in the situation where one is ministering.[40]

This sense of openness to the people and the culture where one is ministering is crucial for successful liturgical inculturation. It is also basic to the understanding of ministry that was inspired by Vatican II's concern for the "updating" of the church in the modern world. Ministry, within the liturgy or outside of it, is not a matter of imposing the tradition *as it understood by the minister* on the people and the culture where one is working, as if the minister has all the answers. Rather, it is a question of putting the tradition in dialogue with the lives and the experiences of others in order for all involved to see the movement of God's spirit, which is constantly "making all things new." Thomas Groome, the noted expert in catechesis, describes the reason for this pastoral stance: The Christian faith is dynamic, alive and continues to unfold throughout history.

If pastoral agents perceive Christian revelation as a static and closed expression of the fullness of divine truth, they will oppose genuine dialogue or encounter with their cultural context. Clearly, true inculturation demands the conviction that the "story" of the Christian faith (i.e., all the symbols that express and carry its truth and ethic over time) is still unfolding, that it has depths yet to be fathomed, and a surplus of meaning that will never be exhausted. . . . Agents of inculturation need to be convinced of this "unfolding" sense of Christian faith, as the faith of a pilgrim people.[41]

Pastoral agents, aware of the need for responsible inculturation, will likewise be aware of the need to listen. They will also facilitate the dialogue between the tradition and the culture in such a way that the liturgy will be able to speak more effectively in its cultural context. In order for this dialogue to take place, though, ministers need to be critically aware of the cultural context in which the liturgy is celebrated.

It is also important to understand the dynamic basis for an effective dialogue. Societies are always in a state of change. That is why inculturation will never be accomplished once and for all. There must be a continual reflection and dialogue on the part of Christians to see whether their understanding and presentation of the gospel is still effective in their culture, is still up-to-date, or *aggiornata,* as the Italians would say.

Mindful of the complex tasks involved with inculturating the liturgy—namely, the need to be faithful to the gospel and the received traditions, while at the same time making both intelligible to the people of our culture—we now turn to our own context, the United States.

Notes

1. Adrian Hastings, "Western Christianity Confronts Other Cultures," *Studia Liturgica* 20 (1990): 22.

2. See #53.

3. Among these are Pope Paul VI's important encyclical *Evangelii nuntiandi* (1975), Pope John Paul II's encyclicals *Catechesi tradendae* (1979) and *Redemptoris missio* (1990), and statements from the Pontifical Council for Culture such as *Towards a Pastoral Approach to Culture* (1999).

4. *Ad Petri cathedram, Acta Apostolicae Sedis* (1959): 513. This principle is repeated in *Gaudium et spes,* 92.

5. See also the first article of *Sacrosanctum concilium* (SC), which announces that the overall goal of the Council is "to adapt more suitably to the needs of our times those institutions that are subject to change."

6. See Anscar Chupungco, "Liturgy and Inculturation," *Handbook for Liturgical Studies II: Fundamental Liturgy* (Collegeville, Minnesota: The Liturgical Press, 1998), 361.

7. Anibale Bugnini, *The Reform of the Liturgy, 1948–1975* (Collegeville, Minnesota: The Liturgical Press, 1990).

8. There are many articles written on the various sources for the present Roman sacramentary. For an idea of its hybrid nature see H. Ashworth, "Les sources patristiques du nouveau missel romain," *Questions Liturgiques* 52 (1971): 295–304; F. Brovelli, "Lo studio dell'eucologia," in E. Cattaneo, *Il culto cristiano in occidente,* B.E.L. 13 (Rome: Edizione Liturgiche, 1985), 595–622; Alexandre Dumas, "Pour mieux comprendre les textes liturgiques du missel romaine," *Notitiae* 6 (1970): 194–213; Pierre Jounel, "Sources françaises du nouveau missel romain," *Questions Liturgiques* 52 (1971): 295–304; Thomas Krosnicki, "The New Blessings in the Missal of Paul VI," *Worship* 45 (1971): 199–205; and "The Post-Communion Prayers at the Masses for *Scrutiniis Peragendis,*" *Notitiae* 19 (1983): 145–55.

9. See Enrico Mazza, *The Celebration of the Eucharist: The Origin of the Rite and the Development of Its Interpretation* (Collegeville, Minnesota: The Liturgical Press, 1999), 271–75.

10. For a fuller discussion of this topic see my "The Dialogue Is Just Getting Started: The Roman Liturgy and Inculturation, Nos. 33–37, 46–51," *Pastoral Music* 19:5 (June–July 1995): 35–39.

11. Anscar Chupungco has long maintained the usefulness of looking at inculturation as one approach to the process of cultural adaptation. See his "Liturgical Inculturation," *East Asian Pastoral Review* 30 (1993): 110.

12. It is clear that if this document were written today, the authors would be very comfortable with substituting the word "inculturation" for "adaptation" in many instances. See Anscar Chupungco's lucid overview of this question in his article "A Definition of Liturgical Inculturation," *Ecclesia Orans* 5 (1988): 11–23; see also his "Liturgy and Inculturation," in A. J. Chupungco, ed., *Handbook for Liturgical Studies II: Fundamental Liturgy* (Collegeville, Minnesota: The Liturgical Press, 1997), 337–75.

13. J. Masson, "L'Église ouverte sur le monde," *Nouvelle Revue Théologique* 84 (1962): 1038.

14. Aylward Shorter, *Toward a Theology of Inculturation* (Maryknoll, New York: Orbis Books, 1988), 5.

15. On the nuances of each of these terms, see Anscar Chupungco, *Liturgical Inculturation: Sacramentals, Religiosity, and Catechesis* (Collegeville, Minnesota: The Liturgical Press, 1992), 13–32.

16. "Address to the Pontifical Biblical Commission," *Fede e cultura alla luce della Bibbia* (Torino: Elle di Ci, 1981), 5.

17. See for example G. Arbuckle, "Inculturation Not Adaptation: Time to Change Terminology," *Worship* 60 (1986): 519. The change of preferred vocabulary from "adaptation" to "inculturation," especially in reference to the liturgy, was made official in *Varietates legitimae* (VL), 4.

18. The first description of inculturation that relates it to the incarnation is found in Vatican II's decree *Ad gentes* (on the missionary activity of the church), 22: "Just as happened in the economy of the incarnation, the young churches, which are rooted in Christ and built on the foundations of the apostles, take over all the riches of the nations which have been given to Christ as an inheritance (cf. Ps. 2:8)."

19. See John Paul II's opening address to the Pontifical Council for Culture, *The Pope Speaks* 27 (1982): 157.

20. See *Redemptoris missio* (RM), 52.

21. VL, 4, speaks of this double movement of inculturation and relates this movement to the incarnation.

22. See Anscar Chupungco, "A Definition of Liturgical Inculturation," 11–23.

23. Paul Verlaine, "Chanson d'automne," in George Pompidou, ed., *Anthologie de la Poésie française* (Paris: Hachette, 1971), 427. This poem was read over the BBC the evening before the Normandy invasion in order to indicate to the French underground that D-Day was about to commence.

24. See *Comme le prévoit* (CP), 28; also H. Leclercq, "Cursus" in *Dictionnaire d'Archéologie Chrétienne et de Liturgie,* 3: 3193–205.

25. See the very helpful article on this and other difficulties related to translation by Alexandre Dumas, "Pour mieux comprendre les textes liturgiques du missel romain," Notitiae 6 (1970): 194–213.

26. Cyrille Vogel, "The Cultic Environment of the Deceased in the Early Christian Period," *Temple of the Holy Spirit* (Collegeville, Minnesota: The Liturgical Press), 259–76.

27. See also *General Instruction of the Roman Missal,* 53.

28. For two excellent articles on liturgical translation in general see Mattias Augé, "Principi di interpretazione dei testi liturgici," in S. Marsili et al, eds., *Anàmnesis 1: La Liturgia: Momento nella storia della salvezza* (Casale Monferrato: Marietti, 1974), 74–178, and Anscar Chupungco, "The Translation of Liturgical Texts," *Handbook for Liturgical Studies I: Introduction to the Liturgy* (Collegeville, Minnesota: The Liturgical Press, 1997), 381–97.

29. Conférence Épiscopal de Zaïre, *Rite Zaïrois de la célébration eucharistique* (Kinshasa, 1985), 44–45. On this inculturated version of the Roman rite see also Congregatio Pro Culto Divino, "Le missel romain pour les diocèses du Zaïre," *Notitiae* 24 (1988): 454–72; Chris Nwaka Egbulem, "An African Interpretation of Liturgical Inculturation: The Rite *Zairois*," in M. Downey and R. Fragomeni, eds., *A Promise of Presence* (Washington: Pastoral Press, 1992), 227–50; and R. Moloney, "The Zairean Mass and Inculturation," *Worship* 62 (1988): 433–42. Finally, see also F. Kabasele Lumbala's overview of not only the Zaire liturgy but also of developments in Cameroon and Malawi, and the issue of using native food and drink for the eucharistic elements in *Celebrating Jesus Christ in Africa* (Maryknoll, New York: Orbis Books, 1998), 24–57.

30. Robert J. Schreiter, *Constructing Local Theologies* (Maryknoll, New York: Orbis Books, 1985), 2.

31. Anscar Chupungco, "A Definition of Liturgical Inculturation," 22.

32. H. Richard Niebuhr, *Christ and Culture* (New York: Harper and Row, 1951).

33. See Geoffrey Wainwright's exposition and explanation of these models in *Doxology: The Praise of God in Worship, Doctrine and Life* (New York: Oxford University Press, 1980), 384–98, and John Witvliet, "Theological and Conceptual Models for Liturgy and Culture," *Liturgy Digest* 3 (1996): 5–46. For a fascinating application of the Niebuhr typologies see James White, "Worship and Culture: Mirror or Beacon?" *Theological Studies* 35 (1974): 288–301. For a fine historical overview of the different images of Christ throughout (Western) history, see Jaroslav Pelikan, *Jesus through the Centuries: His Place in the History of Culture* (New York: Harper and Row, 1987).

34. These dynamic relationships are explored in a document prepared in 1996 called the "Nairobi Statement on Worship and Culture: Contemporary Challenges and Opportunities," *LWF Studies 1/1996: Christian Worship: Unity in Cultural Diversity* (Geneva, Switzerland: Lutheran World Federation, 1996): 23–28. See also a previous publication containing the papers from the two previous consultations, *LWF Studies 3/1994: Worship and Culture in Dialogue* (Geneva, Switzerland: Lutheran World Federation, 1994).

35. RM, 52.

36. See the details of this racist request in Mark Searle, "Culture," in *Liturgy: Active Participation in the Divine Life* (Collegeville, Minnesota: The Liturgical Press, 1990), 27–51.

37. I am indebted to Peter Schineller for these ideas, which I have adapted for purposes of discussing liturgical inculturation. For his original treatment of this, see his *A Handbook on Inculturation* (New York: Paulist Press, 1990), 61–73. Also, see Stephen Bevans's presentation, which uses this concept as a backdrop for his models of contextualization (inculturation), in *Models of Contextual Theology* (Maryknoll, New York: Orbis Books, 1992), 23–29. I have simplified the schema for the sake of brevity.

38. See SC, 11.

39. Schineller, *A Handbook on Inculturation,* 69.

40. *Ibid.,* 69, 70.

41. Thomas Groome, "Inculturation: How to Proceed in a Pastoral Context," in Greinacher and Mette, eds., *Christianity and Cultures, Concilium* 1994/2: 120–33.

Chapter Five

Inculturation of the Liturgy in the United States

It may strike some as inappropriate to speak of inculturating the liturgy in the United States. There would be little argument that the way Catholics worship in an Asian culture needs to be appreciably different than the way Catholics worship in Rome. However, there are some who argue that because the United States is basically a Western country with a long association with Christianity there is no need to inculturate our worship. In part, this is true. However, if a community celebrates the rite exactly as it is presented in the liturgical books without implementing the many ways the rite itself calls for pastoral adaptation, that community is being unfaithful to the spirit of the liturgical renewal and missing an opportunity to make their liturgy truly living worship. Why? Because the *editiones typicae* issued by Rome and translated and adapted into English are not just new, updated versions of the Tridentine missal. That liturgical book, as we have seen, allowed absolutely no concession to local variation. Rather, the liturgical books resulting from Vatican II's reform of the liturgy are presented to local churches to be adapted to local situations—even if those churches happen to be rooted culturally in European expressions of the faith.

A Look at Culture in the United States

It is beyond the scope of this book to offer a comprehensive analysis of the U.S. cultural scene. But as we take a look at our own society it is important to remember a caveat already voiced: No culture is totally Christian; no culture is perfectly evangelized. All cultures— even those that are considered "Christian"—regularly need to have their values and institutions evaluated in light of the gospel. For this reason, Pope John Paul II, in continuity with the teaching of Paul VI, has called for a "new evangelization" that is directed not simply to individuals but to whole cultures.[1]

What can be said specifically of U.S. culture? This is an extremely complex question. It is more correct to speak of U.S. *cultures*—in the plural—since with each passing year the population of the United States is becoming more and more multicultural. It is also obvious that there are definite regional cultural differences in the United States that are signaled by, but go beyond, the way English is spoken. An African American business executive in Houston, for example, not only speaks English differently from a rural white farmer in Appalachia, but also has a different view of life occasioned by geographic location, economic status and race, among others. Both people, however, are equally American. The issues raised by our multicultural reality, especially in our larger cities, and by the regional differences among Americans challenge generalizations about "U.S. culture." We need always be aware that we can never exhaustively describe the U.S. cultural context because of its complexity.

We also need to be aware that American culture is a kind of moving target; it is changing and reinventing itself constantly not only because of the new groups being added to the cultural mix but also because of the exponential changes in daily life wrought by technology. Just as the automobile profoundly changed U.S. society in the 1920s, so the personal computer has transformed much of U.S. society in the last ten years, affecting how many of us live, communicate with one another and view our world.

Having noted all of these cautions, let us take a brief look at some of the characteristics of what could be called U.S. "mainstream" culture—an umbrella term used to describe the general cultural characteristics shared by the majority of people living in the United States. We will look especially at those characteristics that influence liturgy, for better and for worse.

Religion in the United States: Popular but Private

Visitors from Europe, especially from an ideologically secular country like France, are always struck by the overt references to God and religious belief in the United States. Presidents routinely make reference to God and urge their citizens to pray in times of crisis and national thanksgiving. We take public oaths with a hand on the Bible. The pledge of allegiance states that we are "one nation, under God." U.S. currency prominently bears the declaration "In God We Trust" (yet Americans visiting Rome are often surprised to find a bank named after the Holy Spirit!). According to surveys, most Americans claim to be religious. The United States has the highest level of church attendance in the Western industrialized world.

Does religion really have an effect on how we live? Stephen Carter, in his 1993 bestseller *The Culture of Disbelief: How American Law and Politics Trivialize Religious Devotion,* argues that religious belief has become such a private affair that religion and its guiding moral principals are effectively excluded from any serious discussion of the controversial issues of the day. We are afraid of imposing our beliefs on others. Mainstream U.S. culture sees religion as something Americans voluntarily do on a Sunday—a kind of "religious hobby" that has and should have no bearing on how they come to decisions and live their lives in a multireligious and multicultural society. Carter is not alone in making this observation; other commentators on U.S. culture have noted the same tendency.[2]

Unlike other countries with state churches, the United States has no one religious denomination that is identified with it. This separation of church and state has generally been beneficial to both religion and civil society. Freedom of religion is a cherished American principle, but we pay a price for this freedom. Religion in the United States has largely become a private affair. Many Americans pick and choose their places of worship based less on denominational affiliation than on the particular church's ability to meet their needs. The phenomenal growth of the nondenominational "megachurches" in white suburban areas around the country illustrates the success of this approach. Offering a range of services from baby-sitting to self-help groups, combined with an informal, entertainment-style Sunday service that has no discernable link with a historical tradition of worship, the megachurch is an example of the inculturation of Christianity into American white middle-class culture.

While this style of church has many enthusiastic proponents, there are Catholic and Protestant observers who see the megachurches as an unfortunate impoverishment of the Christian tradition, especially its traditions of worship. At its worst, the megachurch acquiesces to the dominant trends in mainstream American culture that search for the therapeutic and entertaining without a sense of commitment, community and mission that has historically been a part of the Christian faith.[3] These churches flourish because, in the free marketplace of ideas, they have come up with an attractive product. Many wonder whether we are reducing religion to just another commodity like corn flakes and deodorant. R. Laurence Moore, in a trenchant critique of this cultural tendency, has traced its history in his book *Selling God.*[4] The United States, with its strong commercial culture, has long used marketing techniques to sell religion. If the ultimate criterion for maintaining or developing religious practices is "what sells," we are developing a much different kind of faith than the one proclaimed by traditional Christianity.

Postmodernity

Another characteristic of mainstream U.S. culture is that it has entered into what many scholars call the cultural period of "postmodernity." Postmodernity is used to describe the cultural environment in which we now live, the time after "modernity." (Modernity is the period in Western history that began with the Enlightenment in the eighteenth century and ended in the period after World War I.) Subjectivity, individualism and a lack of interest in history are characteristic of postmodern North Atlantic culture in Europe, the United States and Canada.

How does cultural postmodernity see the world?[5] We live in a culture today that questions most of the achievements trumpeted by previous generations. The confidence that science and technology, informed by human reason, will inevitably lead to a better quality of life has been severely shaken. Degradation of the environment caused by a naive sense of technological progress, discredited political systems such as communism that were supposedly inspired by scientific observation about the world and human history, and the terrible disparity between rich and poor nations that seems to be abetted by capitalist economic theory have all seriously challenged the old truths upon which Western assumptions about the world were based.

In addition, postmodern society emphasizes the personal and the subjective over the public and the objective. There is a reluctance in our culture to say we have the "truth," since the truth, especially in a diverse society, appears to be so relative. Much of this reluctance is based on the recognition that differences in culture and background lead to legitimately divergent perceptions of the world.

As a consequence, authority—both civil and religious—is under siege. Institutions like the Roman Catholic church now need to convince individuals that their points of view on the issues that affect human life and public policy are the correct ones.[6] As Michael Paul Gallagher puts it,

> the big claims of modernity have fallen under suspicion and come to be largely rejected, but the "turn to the subject" born with

modernity has not only survived the transition but become an even more crucial strand of our lived culture. . . . According to one judgement we have fallen further into isolation, fragmentation and narcissism, where life is an indifferent game and individual options are merely aesthetic or provisional.[7]

However, there is another, more positive way of seeing post-modernity. Rather than looking at these cultural characteristics as overly subjective and divisive, the development of a new conscious-ness not dominated by an excessive rationalism provides space for God and spirituality that was not possible in the more rationalistic modern period.

[T]he oft-maligned sense of self can be the source of our hope, because permanent hungers of the heart come to expression with new honesty and the quest for liberation and authenticity takes on a new humility. Even the sense of dispersal . . . rebounds into a spiritual search for community and roots. Spirituality becomes not just a fashionable term but a real issue in this era beyond the oppression of modernity.[8]

Catholicism and U.S. Culture

As people of faith, how should Catholics look at U.S. culture? Can the more positive aspects of our culture, such as the spiritual quest for liberation and authenticity, aid the process of responsible incul-turation of the liturgy in the United States? Or does the postmodern insistence on the relative nature of religious experience force us to reject U.S. mainstream culture as a possible context for authentic Christian belief?[9]

In my opinion, it would be a mistake to view our cultural con-text as inimical to faith and liturgy. Clearly our response as believers needs to be much more discerning than a simple siege mentality that seeks to avoid the influence of the postmodern world. That approach would simply return us to the attitude prevalent in the church before Vatican II, discussed in the first chapter of this book. Pope John XXIII, confident that God's grace is at work in the world, offers words of wisdom as appropriate today as they were just before Vatican II:

> In the daily exercise of our pastoral office, we sometimes have to listen, much to our regret, to voices of persons who, though burning with zeal, are not endowed with too much sense of discretion or measure. In these modern times they can see nothing but prevarication and ruin. They say that our era, in comparison with past eras, is getting worse, and they behave as though they have learned nothing from history, which is, nonetheless, the teacher of life. . . . [W]e feel we must disagree with these prophets of gloom, who are always forecasting disaster, as though the end of the world were at hand. In the present order of things, Divine Providence is leading us to a new order of human relations.[10]

What signs of the leadership of divine providence can we discern in U.S. culture? How can the positive aspects of our culture that are in harmony with the gospel help us to inculturate the liturgy in a responsible way?

The Dignity of the Human Person

Perhaps one of the most positive tendencies in American culture is the flip side of postmodern subjectivism and individualism: the deeply-held value of the sanctity of the individual conscience. Flowing from this value is the notion that finding God in our society is often a personal quest that demands personal decisions.[11] Since belonging to a church, any church, is now perceived as largely a matter of choice and not family tradition, personal appropriation of the values of the gospel is a stronger criterion for evaluating church membership today than it has been in the past. Implicit in this development is a challenge to church leaders to make sense to individuals and to present a compelling case for belief in the gospel and participation in the life of the church.

Although at times problematic, the focus on the individual and personal is not necessarily inimical to a renewed liturgy. As Kenneth Smits points out, "[O]ur present liturgical reform is marked by an attention to person and roles that goes beyond the scope of previous

Catholic liturgy. The development of more person-oriented liturgical symbols is manifest in all the new rites. Here, culture and religious values can meet and assist one another."[12]

Given the American emphasis on attending to the individual, it is not surprising that the Rite of Christian Initiation of Adults has been embraced by so many U.S. parishes with an enthusiasm unparalleled in other countries in which Christianity is already well established.[13] In those parishes that have implemented RCIA well, it is not surprising to see that attention to an individual's faith development and appropriation of the tradition through dialogue and personal relationship with other believers is an effective way of initiating the rugged individualists of U.S. culture into the church. The fact that the process takes place in the context of communal prayer helps to attenuate some of the worst aspects of the American "lone ranger" mentality, while allowing people the space and the time to undertake the journey of conversion at their own pace.

A Faith Nurtured by Experience

A personal appropriation of faith is an important aspect of the American experience of religion. As we have seen, this appropriation takes place when the gospel is presented in such a way as it makes sense to the individual in light of their own experience. As the U.S. Bishops' Committee on the Liturgy reminds us, "we do not come to meet Christ [at worship] as if he were absent from the rest of our lives" (*Music in Catholic Worship,* 2). There is always the search for the practical connection between worship and the rest of life. This is important for all Christians, but it seems that it is even more so in the United States since American Catholics tend to look for "theological wisdom in the meaning of concrete experience."[14] Because of our tendency toward pragmatism, philosophy and ideas usually hold little power to persuade us; concepts need to be connected to daily life and translated into action.

Increasingly, middle-class European American Catholics—better educated than their immigrant forebears and engaged in professions such as education, medicine and law—seek church structures that respond to their input and experiences. The Counter-Reformation division of the church into the *ecclesia docens* (the teaching church, the clergy) and the *ecclesia discens* (the learning church, the laity) that held sway before Vatican II makes little sense to most of the post-conciliar generation of American Catholics.[15] The formation of parish (pastoral) councils, encouraged by the *Code of Canon Law*[16] and widely undertaken in the United States, illustrates the way that lay American Catholics have assumed responsibility for the life of their own parishes. Such participation in the life of the parish comes naturally to a people for whom representative democracy is the accepted way that society is structured.

We must also take seriously the fact that American lay Catholics hold a place in the U.S. Catholic church not enjoyed by lay people in other churches around the world. U.S. lay Catholics are generally well educated, and those that work for the church do so as professionals within the official structure of the church. Never before in church history have so many held graduate degrees in theology, ministry and religion. It has not been since the first centuries of the church that so many lay women and men have been involved in active church ministry and active church leadership.[17]

Our liturgical assemblies manifest the many ministerial roles that lay people are now assuming outside the liturgy. Acting as a kind of mirror of the local community, the liturgy reflects the way that parish life and ministry are organized. While maintaining the foundational characteristic of the liturgy as both "hierarchic" and "communal,"[18] American Catholic liturgies feature lay people proclaiming the scriptures, voicing petitions, distributing the eucharist, welcoming other members, and at times offering reflections on scripture, all of which illustrate the call to ministry that Vatican II linked to baptism. No longer does the priest represent the only official face of the church at worship; neither is he the only minister outside the liturgy.

U.S. Catholics have an increasing tendency to see religion and access to God as democratic experiences. One commentator, describing distinctive characteristics of American Catholic spirituality, stated that we "are not impressed by the thought that spiritual gifts are spread around about as unevenly as IQ, health, and length of life."[19] Rather, it is a common conviction among U.S. Catholics that all should have access to the holy. While none of this is without its ambiguities, especially when it comes to the reception of sacraments,[20] it again underlines the American ideal of equal opportunity in all areas of life, religious as well as economic and social. It also renders the current insistence in some quarters on a clerical monopoly on ministry in the church an increasingly problematic and ineffectual solution to carrying out the mission of the gospel.

Feminism and Inclusion of the Marginalized

Another positive witness to gospel values by U.S. culture is the growing awareness of the need to address and redress the inequality and oppression experienced by women. Ever since we realized that our social institutions and the social roles of women and men were not divinely instituted, the place of women in our society has received much attention. Within the past century, U.S. culture has witnessed a profound transformation of the social roles of women. Women now routinely pursue careers in medicine, ministry, law, education, business and the military that were almost exclusively limited to men prior to the twentieth century. While the United States still has a long way to go to remedy completely the systemic second-class social status of women, it has been the international leader in struggling with age-old prejudices that have denied women the same opportunities and respect given their male counterparts.

The drive to ensure the equal treatment of women has become a hallmark of the latter part of the twentieth century and has had repercussions in the way basic structures of society are understood. Not surprisingly, the struggle for equality for women has led to a new sensitivity to others in society that have been set on the margins throughout history. For example, over the past four decades, efforts have been made to further just treatment for people of color, for those with physical and mental disabilities, and for lesbians and gay men.

All of this, to a greater or lesser degree, presents a challenge to how we worship. The use of language that does not denigrate or exclude women or others who have not traditionally held power or fit into the norm of mainstream society is a concern not only of academia, commerce and politics, but also of the church. The intentional opening up of liturgical roles to women and all others who have experienced unjust discrimination likewise reflects the desire of the church in the United States to act justly in light of our acknowledgment that past discriminatory attitudes and divisions come from our human sinfulness rather than divine institution.

Much more could be said about the cultural reality of the United States, but the foregoing discussion situates the challenge that all Christians face in trying to proclaim the gospel effectively and worship faithfully in a constantly evolving cultural context. The task before us is ongoing and complex. On the one hand, we need to be careful in our liturgies lest we capitulate to those aspects of our culture that are not in harmony with the gospel. On the other hand, we must also be careful not to become so rigidly attached to our liturgical tradition that we loose contact with the lived culture and thereby become irrelevant. The task is one that cannot be undertaken alone but only in concert with others as a church. By holding the liturgical tradition, our own particular point of view, and the U.S. cultural context in a constant but productive tension, we will at least be able to ask the questions necessary to continue the process of liturgical inculturation in a responsible way.

Practical Steps toward Inculturation

We will now look at some practical ways that the liturgy can be appropriately inculturated in the United States. Rather than look at individual rites, we will consider the many languages used by the liturgy to communicate the gospel.

Assembly and Ministers

One of the truisms we rediscovered with the liturgical reform of Vatican II is that "books don't do liturgy, *people* do liturgy." What does this mean practically? It means that the identity of those who enact the liturgy—the flesh-and-blood people who carry out the various liturgical roles—needs to be seriously considered when envisioning the rites. It is, after all, the assembly that is the primary subject of the liturgical action, and the assembly exists in a certain time and place, and has a composite cultural identity that affects the way it comes together for worship.

It is often helpful to consider how the assembly gathers to see if it corresponds to the way that we show hospitality outside the liturgy. One's experience of worship begins as one enters the church, well before the first note of the gathering song is sounded. Given the importance our culture attaches to recognizing individuals and their importance, it seems vital that those gathering for worship be welcomed in a warm, personal way. This also corresponds to the best of our liturgical tradition, which sees each human person as a reflection of the divine. Interestingly, the ministry of hospitality (more than the work of ushers, who merely show people to their seats) is a phenomenon particular to parishes in the United States and is a ministry that expresses a positive aspect of our cultural ethos.

It is also important to examine who is fulfilling the various ministries during the liturgy. Are women carrying out all of the roles that are open to them? If the parish is multicultural, has there been an attempt to involve a cross section of the cultural groups that worship regularly together? Have people with disabilities been invited and prepared to minister in the liturgy? Concerns such as these are based on the fact that inculturation of the liturgy is not only a matter of how things are done, but also who does them. A wide cross section of the people of the parish ministering in the liturgical assembly is an eloquent witness to the diversity of the assembly and a reflection of the cultural context in which it worships.

Posture and Gesture

Compared to many cultures, mainstream U.S. culture is rather schizophrenic when it comes to the human body. Advertising campaigns consistently rely on images of fashionable bodies to promote products—even when there is no practical connection between the image and the product. The marketplace is full of items from diet pills to tanning treatments that promise their users a perfect body (which they apparently do not yet have). Despite this, the prevailing North Atlantic cultural tendency is one of discomfort with our bodies. U.S. religious culture tends to understand the body as either irrelevant to the spiritual life or sinful.

The Roman rite, born in a Mediterranean culture, presupposes a very different approach to the body. The classical Roman tradition calls for movements and postures such as processing, standing, bowing, kneeling and sitting. Gestures such as signing ourselves and others with the cross, kissing, striking the breast and praying with hands outstretched are part of the repertoire of the Roman rite. The Roman rite encourages an embodied approach to worship that corresponds to our Catholic theology of sacrament, which sees creation in general and our bodies in particular as basically good and potentially revelatory of God's presence.[21]

It is here, in the way we think of our bodies, that our received liturgical tradition challenges North American cultural trends, which often regard liturgical gesture and movement as superfluous because it is "of the body." For example, how comfortable is a parish in enacting the washing of the feet on Holy Thursday? In many American parishes the substitution of the quick, antiseptic and non-biblical "washing of the hands" for the inconvenient and messy, yet richly symbolic, foot-washing is an illustration of the problem. I have even heard of parishes in which the foot-washing is replaced by a few moments of silence after a brief exhortation by the presider encouraging the assembly to "imagine washing feet." Given Catholic criteria for inculturation, this is a sad impoverishment of the liturgical tradition.

Yet there is evidence that in some parishes a spontaneous attempt at involving the assembly in a more active, embodied style of celebration is taking root. The assembly's posture during the eucharistic prayer is a case in point. In many parishes the members of the assembly stand during all or part of this rather lengthy prayer proclaimed by the presider, and become more actively involved by voicing acclamations throughout the prayer. Although the Appendix to the *General Instruction of the Roman Missal* for the dioceses of the United States directs that the people kneel beginning after the Sanctus until after the Amen of the eucharistic prayer, unless prevented by a lack of space or some other good reason (#21), and because this prayer is the "center and summit of the entire celebration," it seems contradictory to many to maintain the posture of kneeling with its more penitential character.[22] Another example of a kind of "spontaneous inculturation" is the practice of members of the assembly holding hands at the Lord's Prayer. While the appropriateness of this gesture of unity could be debated given that it is followed by the exchange of peace—another gesture of unity—holding hands is a physical, active way for all present to participate in the celebration.[23]

The use of dance and movement has also been a subject of controversy. The use of dance is problematic if it is disassociated from the liturgical action and performed by a troupe of dancers who do not invite the assembly into any participation beyond simple entertainment. However, dance that is done in the context of procession, the preparation of the altar and gifts, and communal song has the potential of opening up our liturgical symbols by presenting them in a more embodied way.[24] What we need to guard against is anything that forces the liturgical assembly to become a passive audience, thereby robbing it of its rightful active role in the liturgy. This temptation to passivity is great in an entertainment-based culture like ours, which encourages us to be passive consumers rather than protagonists of our own cultural expressions, both secular and religious.[25]

Liturgical Space

The design, floor plan, seating arrangements and architecture of our churches can do much either to facilitate or to hinder the full, conscious and active participation of the assembly. Many American parishes are struggling every Sunday with a worship space that works against the participation of the assembly. For example, it is not easy to celebrate the renewed liturgy in a long rectangular building, with rows of fixed pews all facing an elevated sanctuary placed at one end of the building. While this may be the Tridentine arrangement familiar to many European American Catholics, it does little to facilitate the dialogue and interaction between presider, ministers and assembly that is presupposed by the renewed rite of Mass and the other sacraments.

How would an appropriately inculturated liturgical space look? There is no one perfect plan for a church building, since it needs to reflect the particular people who gather there, as well as the place in which they gather. Whatever is planned, the axiom that "the buildings we shape will eventually shape us" should be remembered.[26] Throughout all of Christian history, our places of worship have reflected both cultural and theological values that were judged important for Christian identity.[27] We are now at a point in our development where it is neither necessary nor helpful to slavishly follow the architectural models of the past. Instead, it is more important to build from the view that context is a crucial design criterion. The church building "does not have to 'look like' anything else, past or present. Its integrity, simplicity and beauty, its physical location and landscaping should take into account the neighborhood, city and area in which it is built" (*Environment and Art in Catholic Worship* [EACW], 42).

Another primary criterion for an appropriately inculturated worship space is hospitality: How well does it invite the assembly to gather within its precincts? And how well does it send out those who have gathered to accomplish their mission "to love and serve God." Just as the fourth-century Christian church borrowed the basilican style of architecture, which served as both law court and marketplace, so today church architects in the United States are looking to contemporary civic and commercial buildings for inspiration in designing church buildings.[28] Naturally, it is important to adapt these models critically. In the words of one critic, modern commercial spaces like malls often evoke "escapism and banality."[29] A sense of human scale also needs to be considered when designing new church buildings.

Whatever space is designed, either for a new building or the renovation of an older structure, it is paramount that it allow those gathered to feel that they are a welcome part of a community and to participate easily in the liturgy. The importance of the communal nature of the celebration of the sacraments, especially baptism, also calls on architects and designers of worship spaces to plan for more than just the celebration of the eucharist. There is also a yearning on the part of many for a sacred space that is clearly set apart for meditation, accessible yet away from the bustle and noise of the larger church structure. Blessed sacrament chapels, mandated by the *General Instruction of the Roman Missal* (#276), offer this needed area for quiet and recollection.[30]

Art, Furnishings and Devotional Areas

In our postmodern era, there are few cultural enterprises more subjective than art. In the years immediately following Vatican II, a
certain preference for simplicity in worship spaces severely limited
the number of images in new churches. While this was done out of a
laudable effort to avoid visual distraction and to focus the assembly
on the action of the liturgy, the overall effect for some Catholics was
one of austerity and coldness. We are still learning how to incorpo-
rate images into our worship spaces in such a way as to avoid over-
loading the space and overshadowing the assembly.

Whatever the particular predilection of the local assembly, liturgical art must go beyond the superficial and merely decorative; it
must truly serve the liturgy. It is difficult to find this kind of art in a
catalog of religious goods. Two criteria that offer a helpful starting
point for evaluating art used in the worship space are quality and
appropriateness. "Quality means love and care in the making of something, honesty and genuineness with any materials used, and the
artist's special gift in producing a harmonious whole, a well crafted
work" (EACW, 19). "Appropriateness" has to do with the ability of a
particular work of art to serve the liturgy. It has two components, "[I]t
must be capable of bearing the weight, awe, reverence, and wonder
which the liturgical action expresses; it must clearly serve (and not
interrupt) the ritual action which has its own structure, rhythm, and
movement" (EACW, 21).

While much debate often centers around representational art in
the renovation of older church buildings or the construction of new
churches, more attention to the furnishings that serve as focal points
for the assembly's action would do much to locate the celebration in
the cultural world of the assembly. For example, rather than a large,
marble altar table imported from Italy and bearing little connection to
the people of the assembly, a locally-designed and -constructed altar
could very well be more appropriate from the point of view of both
ecclesiology and liturgical theology. Since the altar-table is an important liturgical symbol of Christ, it "should be the most beautifully

designed and constructed table the community can provide."[31] A locally-crafted altar-table would help people see the connection between their lives and this "table which is holy and sacred to this assembly's action and sharing" (EACW, 71).

Finally, devotional spaces in our churches also need to be considered since they, too, offer an important opportunity for both inculturation and for welcoming members of the parish who do not belong to "mainstream" U.S. culture. Locating these spaces so they enhance rather than distract from the liturgical action is the contemporary challenge.[32] Basic to this challenge is understanding the unspoken model of holiness that is shown to people through devotional articles and spaces. Just as care should be taken in distributing the various liturgical roles across the widest possible racial and cultural spectrum of parish membership, so images of saints, especially in a multicultural parish, need to be equally diverse.

Language: Words of Inclusion

As we saw in the first chapter of this book, the words we use to name reality help create our world by allowing us to see and attend to what we would otherwise overlook. The words we use publicly to speak about God are therefore crucial because the spoken word helps us attend to and remember in an active way who God is and what God has done for us in Jesus Christ. Readings from sacred scripture, prayer texts, preaching, petitions and exhortations all constitute categories of words that are used in worship and are meant to communicate what we believe.

As we noted above in the discussion of American culture, there has been an effort in the United States since the 1950s to be more respectful and inclusive of those segments of the population who historically have been denied full status—women, people of color, persons with disabilities, gay men and lesbians, the poor. Not surprisingly, our language itself has shifted to reflect these new concerns. The U.S. bishops acknowledged this shift in a 1990 document

concerning the translation of the Bible by noting that "some segments of American culture have become increasingly sensitive to
'exclusive language,' i.e., language which seems to exclude the
equality and dignity of each person regardless of race, gender, creed,
age or ability" (*Criteria for the Evaluation of Inclusive Language
Translation of Scriptural Texts Proposed for Liturgical Use,* 1).

In modern American English we no longer can say "men" if we
mean to refer to both men and women. It is no longer considered
appropriate to refer to a person with a disability as if the disability
itself defined the person—for example, by referring to a person con-
fined to a wheelchair as "a cripple" or collectively to people with
disabilities as "the handicapped."

The images that we use to name God have also expanded in
these years. Prior to the 1960s, the image of God held by Christians in
the United States was almost exclusively that of a man with a long
white beard, based on a culturally-conditioned reading of the Bible. It
has only been in the last several decades, with the advent of feminist
biblical scholars and theologians, that this assumption has been
squarely challenged. While the God of Christian revelation described
in the Bible is a personal God, not an impersonal force and therefore
not an "it," modern scholarship has challenged a naive and erro-
neous notion that God must always be envisioned as masculine. In
speaking about the contribution of feminist biblical scholars, the
Pontifical Biblical Commission notes that they have challenged
believers to enrich their image of God based on the scripture texts
themselves:

> The worldview of today, because of its greater attention to the
> dignity of women and to their role in society and in the church,
> ensures that new questions are put to the Biblical text, which in
> turn, occasions new discoveries. Feminine sensitivity helps to
> unmask and correct certain commonly accepted interpretations
> which were tendentious and sought to justify male domination
> of women. . . . The God of the Bible is not a projection of a patri-
> archal mentality. He is Father, but also the God of tenderness
> and maternal love."[33]

The consequences of this new sensitivity to the way we speak about God is obvious. The use of inclusive-language Bible translations at liturgy has been a concern of the U.S. bishops for a number of years. The revised English sacramentary prepared by the International Commission on English in the Liturgy (ICEL) reflects this change in the way it uses words to refer to men and women, as well as to God. For example, many of the classic Latin prayers beginning with the invocation *Deus* ("God") were rendered "Father" in the 1970 translation of the sacramentary to make the invocation less abstract and to specify that the prayer was directed to the first person of the Trinity. This has been corrected in the proposed revised sacramentary to more accurately reflect the Latin and to be sensitive to an overuse of one particular image of God.[34]

Appropriate inculturation demands that the language we use to speak about God also reflect the new sensitivities and more expansive notion of who God is for us as Catholic Christians. In preaching, in composing petitions, in the spontaneous exhortations that are called for in the rites, the use of inclusive language is not simply a trendy thing to do but a matter of good theology, honesty and justice.[35] In their new compositions, the prayers in the revised sacramentary, along with the second revisions of the other ritual books such as the *Order of Christian Funerals,* invoke God with an expanded range of images that goes beyond the usual images contained in the *editiones typicae.* These images are faithful to the Bible and reflect a God who comes to meet us not only in power and awe but also in gentleness and compassion.[36]

Music

As with all art forms, music is especially tied to culture. Perhaps more than any other liturgical language, music has the power to unite the different members of the assembly in praise, thanksgiving and petition. The question of the inculturation of music is essentially the "pastoral judgement" question posed in *Music in Catholic Worship:*

"Does music in the celebration enable these people to express their faith, in this place, in this age, in this culture?" (#39). The answer to this question with respect to a particular piece of music is not simple, for it requires not only an understanding of the theology expressed in the song and the liturgical appropriateness of a piece, but also demands a technical knowledge of music itself.[37]

Liturgical music has evolved since the Second Vatican Council, and the church in the United States is blessed with creative musician-theologians and composers who are giving us a distinctive voice in worship. The challenge of the inculturation of music continues to be one of composing music that is accessible to a diverse assembly and that serves the liturgy rather than forcing it to come to a halt. As with church design, we are still working out how best to accomplish this goal.

In some ways, helping the assembly to sing is a decidedly countercultural activity, given the entertainment model of worship that has become prevalent in many quarters. We rarely sing anywhere else in our society other than in church. MTV and other entertainment media bombard us with music, but fewer of us today sing or play musical instruments than we did a generation ago. Music education, considered secondary by many school boards, has been cut from the curriculum of many of our schools. This lack of a general background in music affects the ability of an assembly to express itself musically. In international gatherings that I have attended, for example, participants from the United States are usually at a disadvantage when the various national delegations are asked to sing. Despite our rich musical heritage, the American delegation usually remains silent.

Despite the lack of a general education in music, the Notre Dame Study of Parish Life conducted in the late 1980s observed a remarkably obvious phenomenon. When music and text appropriate to the occasion and ritual moment were chosen, and when there was competent song-leading and accompaniment, the assembly sang. It seems important, then, to be discerning about the choice of music and to avoid falling into the temptation to select overly sentimental songs that fail to express the challenge of the gospel. Such music may be popular, but its ability to involve the assembly in prayer and its adequacy in proclaiming our faith in Jesus Christ may be seriously deficient. The recommendation of the Milwaukee Symposia of Church Composers is helpful here:

> Those who compose words for the liturgy need to respect
> the contemporary idiom and linguistic development, yet avoid
> its traps. Currents within society work themselves into our
> language; sometimes these are counter to the Christian message
> and revelation. In the United States there is a tendency to over-
> emphasize the individual, to the detriment of our collective
> consciousness. Redemption in the Judeo-Christian tradition is a
> collective, not a private, reality. It is also a hard reality. Conse-
> quently, overly indulgent, sentimental and personalized texts are
> to be avoided.[38]

Liturgical Time

The liturgy communicates in part through time. The rhythm of the liturgical year, as well as the annual commemoration of saints, roots our celebrations in a common experience of the passing of the seasons. When we speak of inculturating the liturgical year we need to be aware that the rhythm of the week and the civil calendar may very well be in conflict with what is presumed by the liturgical year. It is here that we need to decide which aspects of the liturgical year to insist upon in order to maintain this temporal proclamation of the gospel.

A good example of a conflict between the liturgical and secular calendar is found in the period before Christmas. While the liturgical year presumes it to be four weeks of joyous but restrained expecta-tion, the world around the church is celebrating Christmas as if it had already arrived. Christmas parties held before December 25th, Christmas carols heard in stores and on the radio throughout December, decorations put up in commercial districts in November—all say that Christmas is here and so tend to eliminate the religious meaning of the holiday and substitute for it a sense of generalized "good will" coupled with unbridled consumerism. In this instance the stance of the liturgy—that it is Advent—is definitely countercultural.

On the other hand, it would be helpful for the U.S. bishops, the next time they engage in their periodic reassessment of holy days of obligation, to pay more attention to those annual celebrations that elicit a genuine religious response from the faithful. Many Catholics *spontaneously* come to Mass on Thanksgiving Day. This reflects a normal and healthy tendency to want to integrate our national experience with the values of the gospel, and provides us all with an opportunity to challenge our public life as a country with the justice proclaimed by Christ.[39]

The Multicultural Social Reality of the United States

It would be unrealistic to speak of liturgical inculturation without some observations on the multicultural context of the majority of our local assemblies. One of the hallmarks of the church in the United States at the start of the twenty-first century is the increasing cultural diversity of our parishes. Assemblies in Roman Catholic dioceses such as Los Angeles, Chicago and New York celebrate Mass in more than 30 languages every Sunday. The United States now has the third-largest Spanish-speaking population in the world. Chicago has the double distinction of having the second-largest number of both Polish-speaking residents and Greek-speaking residents of any city in the world. Long Beach, California, is home to the second-largest Cambodian population in the world, and East Los Angeles has the most Salvadorans outside the city of San Salvador.

From all indications, the tendency toward multicultural assemblies will only continue. Extrapolating from the 1990 census figures, for example, an article in *Time* magazine predicted that "by the year 2056 . . . the 'average' U.S. resident, as defined by the census statistics, will trace his/her descent to Africa, Asia, the Hispanic world, the Pacific Islands, Arabia—almost anywhere but white Europe."[40]

This demographic change poses an unprecedented set of pastoral and liturgical challenges, even to a church such as the Roman Catholic communion, which has dealt with cultural diversity in this country since the first wave of mass immigration in the 1830s. In the past "national parishes" were the solution to the multicultural makeup of the church. Common until the 1950s, local parishes were set up to minister to the needs of particular cultural groups in their own language and with respect for their particular customs. They often served as havens where new immigrants could maintain their identity in an often hostile society that looked down on foreigners as inferior. Roman Catholic national parishes almost invariably built their own schools, providing both religious and secular instruction to children, often in the language of the mother country. Within a few square blocks in urban areas in the eastern United States, it was not unusual to see several Catholic churches, each caring for a specific ethnic group: Italian, German, Polish, Irish, Hungarian.

The strategy of national parishes, though, is no longer practical as we move into the new millennium. Robert Schreiter points out three reasons why this solution is no longer tenable:

> First of all, when a national parish has served its purpose and the national group has moved out of the neighborhood, it becomes extremely difficult to close the national parish, even when the number of members has dwindled to a point beyond viability. Sentimental reasons will make former members resistant to closing the parish and will often lead to protracted battles between bishop and members. Second, immigrant neighborhoods are often not so homogeneous anymore. An entry level immigrant neighborhood may hold many cultures instead of just a single one. And third, . . . populations are too fluid or mobile to tie their pastoral needs to a single place.[41]

Despite misgivings in some quarters about multicultural groupings of the faithful, it seems that multicultural parishes are here to stay.[42] It is incumbent on pastoral ministers, then, to deal with this reality in the most effective way possible, hopefully serving as catalysts in helping to build Christian communities that are able to embrace cultural diversity as a gift rather than see it as a threat.

Liturgical Inculturation in a Multicultural Context

Inculturation could be regarded as working at cross-purposes in a multicultural setting, since its goal is to help the liturgy become more intelligible to a specific cultural group. While there may be some merit to this observation, any attempt at liturgical inculturation must take into account the assembly, the people who have gathered in Christ's name and who often represent diverse cultures, socioeconomic groups and ages. It is in this context that we need to speak of the cross-cultural aspect of liturgical inculturation in the United States. Each cultural group in a multicultural parish and diocese has something precious to share with every other group: their particular liturgical interpretation and appropriation of the gospel. It is to the extent that we can share these gifts with one another—without suspicion, fear, and desire for control and dominance—that our multicultural liturgies will truly be "a work of the people."[43]

This is, after all, an intrinsic part of the call to justice that we all received when we put on Christ in baptism. The late Sister Thea Bowman eloquently sums up this point:

> The quest for justice demands that I walk in ways that I never walked before, that I talk and think and pray and learn and grow in ways that are new to me. If I'm going to share faith with my brothers and sisters who are Chinese or Jamaican or South African or Winnebago Indian, I've got to learn new ways, new means, new languages, new rituals, new procedures, new understandings, so I can read my brother's heart, so I can hear my sister's call, and I can live justly.[44]

The Goal of Multicultural Worship

In preparing a multicultural celebration, whether a weekly celebration in a small assembly or an occasional worship event in a large parish, the overarching goal is to help each member of the assembly participate fully, actively and consciously in the liturgy. That is to say, the primary goal of worship that happens to be multicultural is no different from a liturgy with a single cultural group: to celebrate what God has done and continues to do for us in the paschal mystery of Jesus Christ.

Surprising perhaps to some, then, the primary purpose of multicultural liturgy is not to celebrate cultural diversity. The priority in all planning should revolve around exploring ways in which all present, despite differences in language, culture, socioeconomic status and level of education, might feel the hospitality of the assembly and the invitation to participate actively in the liturgy. This needs to be kept in mind lest the worship event become fragmented into a series of unrelated components that, while based on the various cultural backgrounds of the members of the assembly, fails to invite everyone into the prayer.

Verbal Proclamation in a Multicultural Assembly

The proclamation and interpretation of the scriptures is central to the Christian tradition of liturgy. Also central to worship are prayer texts such as eucharistic prayers and collects. Every time words are uttered in public—when a text is read or an admonition is given—there will be those who are automatically excluded from the liturgy if they do not understand the language that is used. Sensitivity to this reality in a multicultural assembly calls for a judicious use of words. In preparing the verbal parts of the liturgy, the planning team should be concerned with the following: making the proclamation of God's word and the prayer texts accessible to as many of those gathered as possible; avoiding an unduly long period of time during which a language not known by the majority of the assembly is used;

and incorporating culturally appropriate means of engaging members of the assembly in hearing and reflecting on the sacred text being proclaimed.

It is helpful to first determine the principal or "base" language of the assembly. This is not necessarily the native language of the majority of the members of the congregation, but the language understood by the majority. For example, in a U.S. parish that has large Hispanic, Polish and Korean populations, the language most accessible to the majority of the members of the assembly would probably be English. If this were the case, the base language for most of the verbal proclamations would be English. Short invitations to prayer, responses to the general intercessions, ordinary parts of the service such as the Kyrie and the Sanctus, and other verbal communications easily understood because of their context can be in the languages of the various cultural groups of the parish.

In the case of the proclamation of scripture, especially in an assembly that is bilingual, it is helpful to introduce each reading with a short synopsis in the language not being used for the reading. Complete verbal translations of scripture readings or prayer texts should be avoided since this can be tedious for the majority of the members of the assembly, many of whom are undoubtedly bilingual. Providing printed translations is one strategy for dealing with problems of understanding occasioned by a multilingual assembly. Even there, however, consideration should be given to the fact that having all that is said translated and published in a booklet could frustrate active listening and make the participation aid rather long and complicated to prepare.

Preaching
One of the most challenging aspects of a multicultural celebration is the preaching. As with the rest of the liturgy there is a difference between bilingual or multilingual preaching and preaching that is truly multicultural. Successful multicultural preachers are able to

move back and forth between the major languages of the assembly with parallel homilies that are culturally specific to each group rather than merely translations of the text of the homily. In this way, speaking for a long time in one language is avoided and even those who are able to understand both languages are kept interested. While the base language of the assembly would be the principal one for the homily, preaching in the other languages of the assembly is an important part of acknowledging and respecting the cultures that are represented. Naturally, the possibility of preaching in this manner depends on the linguistic abilities of the preacher. In some parishes, the homily or preaching is prepared by a multicultural team that is also responsible for actually preaching in the various languages of the assembly. Clearly, more leeway and creativity needs to be given when fulfilling this important ministry in a multicultural assembly.[45]

Attending to the Nonverbal

While spoken language is an important way the liturgy communicates, it is far from the only language the liturgy uses. Movement in the form of processions, standing, sitting and kneeling are important ways that a multicultural assembly is invited into the action of the liturgy. Silence is also a way that we communicate at the liturgy. The obvious advantage to these forms of liturgical participation is that they do not depend on translation and can be easily performed by all in the assembly. It is crucial that care be given to these nonverbal elements of worship since they offer the possibility of encouraging the real participation of all the members of the assembly at the same time.[46]

The primary symbols that are used in many Christian liturgical traditions—bread, wine, oil, water, fire—also should be of concern for a multicultural assembly. Again, these symbols need no translation, and if care is given to using them in a lavish way, much will be done to overcome the divisions in the assembly that are automatically engendered by the use of words alone.[47]

Music in a Multicultural Context

Music has the power to unite an assembly in prayer and praise in a way that other liturgical languages do not. Those charged with music ministry should also be aware that music can also divide an assembly. It is romantic nonsense to presuppose that music is a universal language and that it communicates the same thing to everyone regardless of culture. The interpretation given to tempo, key and musical form may vary a great deal from one culture to another. For example, many people from Central America frequently perceive music that is slow as sad, even if the music is in a major key.[48]

For this reason it is important to avoid a simple translation of one musical form—conditioned by its own history and culture—into another language. For example, a German metrical hymn, while suitable for translation into English because of the cultural and linguistic affinity between German and English, usually translates poorly into Spanish. More successful is an *ostinato* style of music popularized by the Taizé community, or music written in a call-and-response structure, which uses a cantor who sings a short line (perhaps alternating between two languages) and then invites the assembly to repeat. Thankfully, a new bilingual and multilingual liturgical repertoire is now being composed to fill this need.[49]

Environment and Art

Another nonverbal liturgical language important to a multicultural celebration is the environment and art of the worship space. The organization of the interior space, attention to seasonal elements, the iconic representation within the space, the vesture for ministers, the placement and design of devotional areas—all of these should be assessed to assure that they are inviting and hospitable to a multicultural assembly. For example, congregations worshiping in older buildings need to consider whether the images of the sacred that are present in the church reflect only the European American religious experience. Do other groups see themselves reflected in the sacred art and furnishing of the church building?

Cultural groups that have a lively devotional life largely drawn from popular religious practice can be a special challenge in this regard. People from Latin America and the Philippines, for example, find much about the worship spaces of the new European American churches to be cold and lifeless. The intense identification of some of these groups with their devotional images needs to be respected in some way in the communal worship space. The use of banners and other portable art displayed for particular celebrations may be the best solution.[50]

European Devotionalism and Popular Religion

Many of the most recent immigrants to the United States come from cultural groups with a Catholicism that has been shaped by centuries of popular religion. The phenomenon of popular religion is prevalent in cultures that were evangelized by the Spanish and Portuguese, and include those of South America and the Philippines. While European American Catholics may see in Hispanic popular religion similarities with the devotionalism widely practiced by European Americans in the years before Vatican II (for example, novenas, forty hours devotions, statues in the home), Hispanic popular religion was never as directly controlled by the clergy as its European and North American counterparts were. Much Hispanic popular religion developed as a parallel to the official channels of ecclesial mediation (such as the Mass and other sacraments).[51] A helpful description of the particularly Hispanic phenomenon of popular religion is offered by Orlando Espín and Sixto García, who describe popular religion as

> the set of experiences, beliefs and rituals which more-or-less
> peripheral human groups create, assume and develop (within
> concrete socio-cultural and historical contexts, and as a response
> to these contexts) and which to a greater or lesser degree
> distance themselves from what is recognized as normative by
> church and society, striving (through rituals, experiences and

beliefs) to find an access to God and salvation which they feel they cannot find in what the church and society present as normative.[52]

The Catholicism practiced by Hispanics and others is sometimes misunderstood by European American Catholics as a simple throwback to pre-Vatican II practices. It is often either dismissed out of hand or understood to be individualistic and subjective, much like its nineteenth- and early-twentieth-century European counterparts. This is unfortunate since Hispanic popular religion, while including elements of European devotionalism, is also rooted in the experience of the indigenous people of the Americas, as well as those of the Africans brought to this continent as slaves. The Virgin of Guadalupe, for example, with her indigenous features, speaks a message of hope to the native peoples defeated by the Spanish conquest. She elicits a different level of identification and emotion in most Mexicans than does Our Lady of Lourdes, with her European appearance and doctrinal message regarding the Immaculate Conception.[53]

The key to the inculturation of the liturgy among Hispanic/Latino peoples, even in multicultural settings, is clearly attending to how popular religious practices shape their religious imagination and expression of the faith.[54] The public nature of much of popular religious practice also opens avenues for the enrichment of the liturgy of mainstream U.S. Catholicism which, much like the Roman liturgy itself, tends toward a certain privatism, abstraction and lack of feeling.

Notes

1. See Robert Schreiter, "The New Evangelization," in S. Bevans and R. Schroeder, eds., *Word Remembered, Word Proclaimed* (Nettetal: Steyler Verlag, 1997), 47.

2. See, for example, Robert N. Bellah, et al., *Habits of the Heart: Individualism and Commitment in American Life* (Berkeley, California: University of California Press, 1985), and Wade Clark Roof, *A Generation of Seekers: The Spiritual Journeys of the Baby Boom Generation* (San Francisco: Harper, 1993).

3. Martin Marty, for example, a noted historian of religion at the University of Chicago, has consistently been critical of these churches. See a provocative study on this topic done by Frank Senn in his *The Witness of the Worshiping Community* (Mahwah, New Jersey: Paulist Press, 1993). See also M. Francis Mannion, "Liturgy and the Present Crisis of Culture," in Eleanor Bernstein, ed., *Liturgy and Spirituality in Context: Perspectives on Prayer and Culture* (Collegeville, Minnesota: The Liturgical Press, 1990), 1–26; see also Gordon Lathrop's thoughtful article "New Pentecost or Joseph's Britches? Reflections on the History and Meaning of the Worship Ordo in the Megachurches," *Worship* 72 (1998): 521–38.

4. *Selling God: American Religion in the Marketplace of Culture* (New York: Oxford University Press, 1994).

5. I am indebted to Michael Paul Gallagher for the following synopsis of postmodernity. See his *Clashing Symbols: An Introduction to Faith and Culture* (London: Dartman, Longman and Todd, 1997): 92–93.

6. On the erosion of the confidence of young Catholics in the institutional church, but not on basic beliefs such as the presence of Christ in the sacraments or the essential mission of the church to help the poor, see William Dinges, Dean Hoge, Mary Johnson and Juan Gonzales, "A Faith Loosely Held: The Institutional Allegiance of Young Catholics," *Commonweal* 125 (July 17, 1998): 13–18.

7. Gallagher, *Clashing Symbols,* 92.

8. *Ibid.,* 93.

9. Cardinal Joseph Ratzinger critiques the relativism of postmodern North Atlantic society because of its inability to search for transcendental truth. The cardinal seems to imply that this inability renders First World culture incapable of serving as a context for authentic Christianity. See his "Christ, Faith and the Challenge of Cultures," *Origins* 24 (March 30, 1995): 679–86.

10. Speech of October 11, 1962, in *The Documents of Vatican II,* Walter Abbot, ed. (London: Geoffrey Chapman, 1966), 712.

11. See Wade Clark Roof's fascinating study of seven baby boomers, each of whom has personally wrestled with belief and belonging: *A Generation of Seekers: The Spiritual Journeys of the Baby Boom Generation* (San Francisco, California: Harper, 1993).

12. Kennth Smits, "Liturgical Reform in Cultural Perspective," *Worship* 50 (1976): 106.

13. See the discussion of this American acceptance of the RCIA by Balthasar Fischer, one of the European scholars largely responsible for its development: "The Rite of Christian Initiation of Adults: Rediscovery and New Beginnings," *Worship* 64 (1990): 98–106.

14. Joseph A. Tetlow, "The Emergence of an American Catholic Spirituality," *Theological Digest* 40 (1993): 34–35.

15. See Paul Philibert, "The Maturing Face of the Church: Signs of Development and Promise," in T. Fitzgerald and M. Connell, eds., *The Changing Face of the Church* (Chicago: Liturgy Training Publications, 1998), 126–47.

16. See the 1983 *Code of Canon Law,* canon 536.

17. See R. Scott Appleby, "Keeping the Faith in an Age of Extremes," E. Bernstein and M. Connell, eds., *Traditions and Transitions* (Chicago: Liturgy Training Publications, 1998), 60–73.

18. See the Constitution on the Sacred Liturgy *Sacrosanctum concilium,* 26–32.

19. Tetlow, 34.

20. See John Huels, who legitimately challenges the "democratization" of the requirements governing the conferral of anointing of the sick in "Who May Be Anointed," *Disputed Questions in the Liturgy Today* (Chicago: Liturgy Training Publications, 1988), 91–99.

21. On movement and gesture see *Environment and Art in Catholic Worship* (EACW), 55–62. From an African perspective, see Elochukwu Uzukwu, "Human Gestural Behavior as Ritual and Symbolic," *Worship as Body Language* (Collegeville, Minnesota: The Liturgical Press, 1997), 1–40.

22. On the range of movements and gestures in our tradition, see John B. Leonard and Nathan Mitchell, *The Postures of the Assembly during the Eucharistic Prayer* (Chicago: Liturgy Training Publications, 1994), and Richard McCarron, *The Eucharistic Prayer at Sunday Mass* (Chicago: Liturgy Training Publications, 1997), 86–102.

23. Mark R. Francis, "Holding Hands at the Our Father: U.S. Liturgical Inculturation?" *Liturgy 90* (January 1993): 4–7, 15.

24. See Carla deSola, "Liturgical Dance: State of the Art," *Liturgical Ministry* 6 (Spring 1997): 49–57.

25. See Michael Warren, *Communication and Cultural Analysis: A Religious View* (Westport, Connecticut: Bergin and Garvey, 1992), and Neil Postman, *Amusing Ourselves to Death: Public Discource in the Age of Show Business* (New York: Viking Penguin, 1985).

26. See Richard Vosko, "Worship Environments: Between No More and Not Yet," in E. Bernstein and M. Connell, eds., *Traditions and Transition* (Chicago: Liturgy Training Publications, 1998), 178.

27. See S. Anita Stauffer, "Inculturation and Church Architecture," *Sudia Liturgica* 20 (1990): 70–80.

28. See Marchita Mauck, *Shaping a House for the Church* (Chicago: Liturgy Training Publications, 1990), especially 16–23. See also Ira G. Zepp, Jr., *The New Religious Image of Urban America, The Shopping Mall as Ceremonial Center* (Westminster, Maryland: Christian Classics, Inc., 1986).

29. Mauck, *Shaping a House for the Church,* 21–22.

30. See Pope Paul VI, *Eucharisticum mysterium,* 53, *Acta Apostolicae Sedis* 59 (1967): 568; also see *The Roman Ritual,* "Holy Communion and Worship of the Eucharist outside Mass," Introduction (1974; English edition), 9.

31. See *General Instruction of the Roman Missal* (GIRM), 259–70; Appendix to GIRM, 263.

32. See John Buscemi, *Places for Devotion* (Chicago: Liturgy Training Publications, 1993).

33. Pontifical Biblical Commission, "The Interpretation of the Bible in the Church," *Origins* 23 (January 6, 1994): I, E, 2, page 509.

34. On the use of inclusive language in the new sacramentary see James Schellman, "A Look at the New Sacramentary," in E. Bernstein and M. Connell, eds., *Traditions and Transitions,* 129–30.

35. See John Huels, "Liturgy, Inclusive Language, and Canon Law," in K. Hughes and M. Francis, eds., *Living No Longer for Ourselves: Liturgy and Justice in the Nineties* (Collegeville, Minnesota: The Liturgical Press, 1991), 138–52. A practical guide to the whole question is provided by Ronald Witherup, *A Liturgist's Guide to Inclusive Language* (Collegeville, Minnesota: The Liturgical Press, 1996).

36. See for example the way God is invoked in many of the original "Prayers and Texts in Particular Circumstances" in the *Order of Christian Funerals,* 398: "O God, to whom mercy and forgiveness belong" (#12); "Lord God, source and destiny for our lives (#28); "Lord God, giver of all that is true and lovely and gracious" (#33).

37. See *Music in Catholic Worship,* 23–41.

38. *The Milwaukee Symposia for Church Composers: A Ten-Year Report* (Chicago: Liturgy Training Publications, 1992), 53.

39. See John Baldovin, "The Liturgical Year: Calendar for a Just Community," in E. Bernstein, ed., *Liturgy and Spirituality in Context: Perspective on Prayer and Culture* (Collegeville, Minnesota: The Liturgical Press, 1990), 98–113.

40. Naushad Mehta, Sylvester Monroe and Dan Winbush, "Beyond the Melting Pot," *Time Magazine* 135 (April 9, 1990): 38.

41. Robert Schreiter, "Ministry for a Multicultural Church," *Origins* 29 (May 20, 1999): 4. Schreiter also notes that the Australian bishops, facing waves of Asian immigrants after World War II, sent a delegation to the U.S. in order to study possible strategies for ministering in a multicultural setting. The group returned with a recommendation that national parishes not be adopted because of the problems they eventually pose to the wider church.

42. Orlando Espín, "A Multicultural Church? Theological Reflections from Below," in W. Cenkner, ed., *The Multicultural Church: A New Landscape in U.S. Theologies* (New York: Paulist, 1996), 54–71.

43. On some practical guidelines for multicultural liturgy, see Mark R. Francis, *Guidelines for Multicultural Celebrations* (Washington, D.C.: FDLC, 1998).

44. Thea Bowman, FSPA, "Justice, Power, and Praise," in Edward M. Grosz, ed., *Liturgy and Social Justice* (Collegeville, Minnesota: The Liturgical Press, 1989), 37.

45. On oral communication across cultures, see John Condon and Fathi Yousef, "Language and Culture" in *An Introduction to Intercultural Communication* (New York: Macmillan, 1975), 168–96.

46. On the importance of gesture and ritual see Elochukwu Uzukwu, "Human Gestural Behavior as Ritual and Symbolic," in his *Worship as Body Language* (Collegeville, Minnesota: The Liturgical Press), 1–40.

47. On attending to the full symbolic nature of liturgical communication see Mark Francis, *Liturgy in a Multicultural Community* (Collegeville, Minnesota: The Liturgical Press), 49–65.

48. See Linda O'Brien-Rohe's insightful article "Music in a Multicultural Parish," *Liturgical Life* (May-June 1993) (a publication of the Archdiocese of Los Angeles).

49. See Bob Hurd, "Music for Multicultural, Multilingual Liturgy: Theology, Issues and Strategies," *Liturgical Ministry* 6 (1997): 120–33, and Mary Frances Reza, "Cross-Cultural Music Making," *Liturgical Ministry* 3 (1994): 164–69.

50. On liturgical art and culture see Anita Stauffer, "Inculturation and Church Architecture," *Studia Liturgica* 20 (1990): 70–80; on devotions and liturgical environment see John Buscemi, *Places for Devotion.*

51. On the relation between European devotionalism and Hispanic popular religion see my "Building Bridges between Liturgy, Devotionalism and Popular Religion," *Assembly* 20 (April 1994): 636–38.

52. Orlando O. Espín and Sixto J. García, "Hispanic-American Theology," in *Catholic Theological Society of America Proceedings* 42 (1987): 115.

53. See Virgilio Elizondo, *La Morenita, Evangelizer of the Americas* (San Antonio: MAAC, 1976).

54. On the relationship of liturgy to popular religion see Mark Francis and Arturo Pérez-Rodriguez, *Primero Dios: Hispanic Liturgical Resource* (Chicago: Liturgy Training Publications, 1997), V. Elizondo and T. Matovina, *Mestizo Worship: A Pastoral Approach to Liturgical Ministry* (Collegeville, Minnesota: The Liturgical Press, 1998); Orlando Espín, *The Faith of the People: Theological Reflections on Popular Catholicism* (Maryknoll, New York: Orbis, 1997); and James Empereur, "Popular Religion and the Liturgy," *Liturgical Ministry* 7 (1998): 105–20.

Conclusion

On my way to work every day I pass the impressive Field Museum of Natural History, located on Lake Shore Drive in Chicago. This building's neoclassical façade resembles an ancient Greek temple and lends a note of classical elegance to both the Chicago lakefront and the new "museum campus" created to bring together the Field Museum, the Adler Planetarium and the Shedd Aquarium/Oceanarium into a unified park.

The Field Museum and the Shedd Aquarium were built in the early 1900s during an international revival of classical architecture called Beaux-Arts classicism. This architectural style originated in Paris and became popular throughout Europe and beyond. Due to European colonial expansion around the world, new public buildings from Helsinki to Cape Town, from Sao Paulo to Hong Kong, were constructed in this style derived from forms first developed in classical Greece and Rome. Beaux-Arts classicism was naturally favored by the designers of the buildings of the 1893 Columbian Exposition in Chicago, which celebrated the 400th anniversary of Columbus's coming to America. Balanced, massive, self-satisfied and serene, these buildings seem to speak of the timelessness of European cultural forms, now transplanted to the shores of a lake in the "New World."

While the architecture of the Field Museum remains the same to this day, an interesting way of advertising current exhibitions has developed over the last several years. Rather than large signs being placed in front of the museum, the upper space between the columns is now used as an area to hang colorful banners that announce special displays of dinosaur fossils, exhibitions of ancient Egyptian artifacts, or a celebration commemorating the centenary of Philippine independence. These banners, hung in such a way that some protrude in front of the columns, seem to jump out at the viewer, and contrast sharply with the perfect order and symmetry of the classical Greek architecture. A building that for some would be cold, austere and forbidding is made accessible and inviting by this transformation of its façade.

These banners seem to me to be an apt metaphor for the inculturation of the liturgy. The clarity, balance and refinement of the Roman rite, while beautiful from a certain perspective, often needs to be made more open and accessible to the people who use it. It needs to be made "their own" in order for it to communicate the hospitality that we claim as an intrinsic part of good liturgy. There may be purists who object to the modifications made either to the austere classical façade of the museum or to the "Roman genius" of the liturgy in order to make both more inviting and accessible to people at the start of the twenty-first century. Ultimately, however, these changes are crucial for the continuing mission of both the museum and the liturgy. If either are perceived as too cold, remote or austere—out of touch with the world around them— they will both become isolated and detached monuments, visited only by an elite few.

The purpose of this book was to examine how a living tradition of worship such as the Roman rite might be adapted to speak more eloquently the gospel of Jesus Christ to the culturally diverse peoples of the United States. In the first three chapters we saw that culture is an intrinsic part of the experience of being a human being, and that culture naturally shapes the way we see and understand God, one another and the world. We also saw that it is natural that the liturgy, as a product of culture, has been adapted and shaped throughout the church's history and that the Roman rite still carries traces of the cultures of many of the peoples who celebrated it.

In chapter four we reviewed the conscious decision of the bishops of Vatican II to bring the practices of Catholicism, especially our liturgical expression of faith, into dialogue with the many cultures of humanity after almost four centuries of isolating the official prayer of the church from the "corruption" of the modern world. We also saw how this decision was implemented after the Council and the complex nature of the process of liturgical inculturation and the admission of new cultural elements into Roman Catholic worship.

Finally, in chapter five we looked at the multicultural and postmodern reality of the United States, and offered some observations about challenging and renewing this reality in light of the gospel. We then suggested ways in which this renewed reality can in turn influence our American Catholic liturgical practice. The tendency that mainstream U.S. culture has to trivialize religion and religious commitment by reducing it to a consumer good challenges the integrity of traditional Christianity and weakens the ability of the liturgy to speak meaningfully of the paschal mystery. In U.S. society, the private needs of the individual are considered paramount, and common sense seems to dictate that we discard a particular faith or religious affiliation if it no longer serves a purpose for the individual. Our postmodern culture, in exalting subjectivity and independence from history and tradition, has also left us very much alone. While many are in a sincere search for interpersonal relationships and community, that search is elusive, since such connections require some degree of voluntary relinquishment of what many Americans believe to be the primary "good"—namely, absolute freedom. But as theologian David Hollenbach has observed,

> Freedom's most important meaning is *positive,* the ability to shape one's life and one's environment in an active creative way, rather than the negative state of privacy or being left alone by others. For the ancient Greeks, privacy was a state of deprivation, a fact echoed in the etymological link of privacy and privation. Similarly the biblical understanding of freedom, portrayed in the account of the Exodus, is not simply freedom *from constraint* but

> freedom *for participation* in the shared life a people. Liberation is from bondage into community.[1]

This is why common worship as an authentic expression of community is so crucial not only for the Catholic church in the United States but for the larger U.S. society, which is often unable to offer a vision of society larger than an individual's likes and dislikes. One of the basic preconditions for the celebration of liturgy is the acceptance of God's call to form a community, to be a church. The call to live, serve and worship with others who have experienced Jesus Christ is the ultimate answer to our quest for meaning and life.

It is for this reason that the inculturation of the liturgy is such an important ongoing enterprise. In order for our liturgical tradition to "compellingly convoke" us as church by speaking meaningfully of Jesus Christ to the people of our day, it must not only critique the dominant culture, but must also respect and encourage its positive characteristics. These positive aspects include the importance of a faith that is formed not by hierarchical fiat but through personal experience and commitment, the drive for women's dignity and equality, and the inclusion of those who are excluded because of unjust discrimination based on race, disability, sexual orientation or economic status.

We mentioned the cultural sea change in the church in the United States that must, because of its scope and attendant urgent needs, modify the way we express our Catholic faith in worship as we move into the third millennium. The multicultural challenge to the dominant European American culture offers the U.S. church an unprecedented opportunity to move beyond the narrowness of the privatized individualism that affects so much of U.S. life and open itself to the the movement of the Spirit in other cultures and from other perspectives. Many of these cultures, if they are respected and cherished as the gift from God that they are, can show us the way to a more authentic community life, mindful of the daily presence of God in creation and human relationships.

For this to happen, though, we all must develop a listening heart. We need to support the efforts of those who seek to find a liturgical voice that expresses their experience of faith rooted in culture and that is also authentically Catholic. We need to listen, for example, to those who cry out for recognition and for the freedom to worship within the Roman rite in a way that recognizes their cultural gifts. Eva Marie Lumas, in speaking for the African American Catholic community, could be voicing a common concern of many sectors of the U.S. church:

> The current liturgical norms of the Roman rite do not meaningfully recognize or encourage the full spirit and truth of the Black Catholic community. We will never be satisfied with singing Black songs at a liturgy that will not allow us to embody fully our faith in our prayer. We are not content with placing our artifacts around the altar when our prayer texts do not enable us to recognize the victory on the altar that God has won through us. We are not willing to be forced into the confines of Eurocentric religiosity, because we believe our Black religiosity is also a worthy instrument of the living God. And no repackaging of the Vatican II documents can stop our determination to help develop the multicultural potential of the Roman rite.[2]

It seems that my original metaphor of the colorful advertisements in front of the Field Museum needs to be complemented by another metaphor, again drawn from that group of museum buildings I pass each day. Sometimes new conditions and new needs require new and contrasting additions to old buildings. This is the case of the neoclassical Shedd Aquarium. The decision to expand this octagonal classical building in order to be able to house saltwater marine animals led to the construction of an ultramodern glass extension that forms a semicircle around the back of the building, which faces Lake Michigan. No attempt was made to make this addition conform to the neoclassical character of the rest of the building, but the contrast and form of the addition harmoniously blend with what was built a century earlier and serves as a means of housing marine creatures that no one would have dreamed of trying to bring to a city in the middle of the North American continent when the original building was constructed. New needs dictate new forms that are in harmony with the past but are not stifled by it.

One of the overarching goals of the Second Vatican Council was to renew the church at worship in such a way that it would be in touch with the aspirations of modern humanity and more sensitive to the way the Spirit is moving in the world today. The Council set in motion our modern dialogue with culture. It was convoked by the ever optimistic Pope John XXIII. "Good Pope John" once said that he regarded the church not as a dusty museum to be preserved but as a living garden to be cultivated. It is this living, organic and sometimes messy vision that guides the work of liturgical inculturation.

Notes

1. David Hollenbach, SJ, "The Common Good in a Divided Society," *The Santa Clara Lectures* 5 (1999): 6. See also the National Conference of Catholic Bishops, *Economic Justice for All* (Washington, D.C.: NCCB, 1986), 36.

2. Eva Marie Lumas, "Choosing the Better Part: Liturgy, Black and Catholic," *Liturgy 90* (July, 1999): 7.

Pastoral Resources

The following is a list of annotated resources that provide further reading in the area of faith, culture and liturgical inculturation. The list is far from exhaustive but will direct the reader to a broader range of studies on the topic.

Documents

The Catechetical Documents: A Parish Resource. Chicago: Liturgy Training Publications, 1996. A source for Paul VI's apostolic exhortation *Evangelii nuntiandi* (on evangelization in the modern world), December 8, 1975.

Flannery, Austin, ed. *Vatican Council II: The Basic Sixteen Documents.* Northport, New York: Costello Publishing Company, 1996. Contains all of the constitutions, decrees and declarations of Vatican II in a completely revised translation in inclusive language.

International Commission on English in the Liturgy, *Documents on the Liturgy, 1963–1979: Conciliar, Papal, and Curial Texts.* Collegeville, Minnesota: The Liturgical Press, 1982. A source for the following documents: Vatican Council II, constitution *Sacrosanctum concilium* (on the sacred liturgy), December 4, 1963; Consilium, instruction *Comme le prévoit* (on the translation of liturgical texts for celebration with a congregation), January 25, 1969; and *General Instruction of the Roman Missal, 1975.*

John Paul II, encyclical *Redemptoris missio* (on the permanent validity of the church's missionary mandate), in *Origins* 20 (January 31, 1991): 542–68.

The Liturgy Documents: A Parish Resource, Volume One, 3rd ed. Chicago: Liturgy Training Publications, 1991. A source for the following documents: Vatican Council II, constitution *Sacrosanctum concilium* (on the sacred liturgy), December 4, 1963; *General Instruction of the Roman Missal,* 1975; National Conference of Catholic Bishops, Bishops' Committee on the Liturgy, *Music in Catholic Worship,* 1972, 1983; and National Conference of Catholic Bishops, Bishops' Committee on the Liturgy, *Environment and Art in Catholic Worship,* 1978.

The Liturgy Documents: A Parish Resource, Volume Two. Chicago: Liturgy Training Publications, 1999. A source for the following documents: Consilium, instruction *Comme le prévoit* (on the translation of liturgical texts for celebration with a congregation), January 25, 1969; and Congregation for Divine Worship and the Discipline of the Sacraments, instruction *Varietates legitimae* (Inculturation and the Roman Liturgy), January 25, 1994.

Pontifical Biblical Commission, *The Interpretation of the Bible in the Church,* in *Origins* 23 (January 6, 1994): 498–524.

Pontifical Council for Culture, *Towards a Pastoral Approach to Culture,* in *Origins* 29 (June 17, 1999): 65–84. Also available from the United States Catholic Conference, Washington, D.C., and the Vatican website: www.vatican.va/roman_curia/pontifical_councils/cultr.

General Works on Faith and Culture

Arbuckle, Gerald. *Earthing the Gospel: An Inculturation Handbook for Pastoral Workers.* Maryknoll, New York: Orbis Books, 1990. The author is a priest from New Zealand who is also an anthropologist. Written for the nonspecialist pastoral minister in mind, it is full of helpful illustrations and examples of the relationship between faith and culture.

Bevans, Stephen. *Models of Contextual Theology.* Maryknoll, New York: Orbis Books, 1992. An insightful presentation of five different starting points for the inculturation of the faith and the consequences for each of the models. An important work for those who wish to delve more deeply into the practical outcomes of one's theological presuppositions about inculturation.

Bibby, Reginald. "Mosaics and Melting Pots in Motion: Reading and Responding to New Times." *Missiology* 21 (1993): 412–28. A discussion of the complex issues raised by the official policy of multiculturalism in Canada. This article raises important considerations for the U.S. context as well.

Carter, Stephen. *The Culture of Disbelief: How American Law and Politics Trivialize Religious Devotion.* New York: Basic Books, 1993. A fascinating and readable critique of American culture by a professor of law at Yale University. These pages argue convincingly that having public religion is not the same as taking religion seriously.

Cenker, William, ed. *The Multicultural Church: A New Landscape in U.S. Theologies.* New York: Paulist Press, 1995. This collection of essays treats the complicated question of faith in the context of the U.S. multicultural reality. Of special interest is an alternate point of view on multiculturalism presented by Orlando Espín and a fine summary of theological approaches to inculturation by Peter Phan.

Dulles, Avery. "Catholicism and American Culture: The Uneasy Dialogue." *America* 162 (January 27, 1990): 54–59. This noted author of *Models of the Church* presents four Catholic reactions to U.S. culture. A good review of many of the major issues and personalities in the debate concerning culture and faith.

Fitzpatrick, Joseph. *One Church, Many Cultures: The Challenge of Diversity.* Kansas City: Sheed and Ward, 1987. Writing for the nonspecialist from the perspective of the church in the United States, the author presents an engaging history of the interplay between culture and faith. This would be a good place to start for those just beginning a study of faith and culture in the United States.

Gallagher, Michael Paul. *Clashing Symbols: An Introduction to Faith and Culture.* London: Dartman, Longman & Todd, 1997. A professor at the Gregorian University in Rome, the author presents a lucid overview of the major theological and philosophical issues surrounding a consideration of faith and culture. Of special interest is a presentation of the effects of postmodernity on the church and on the presentation of the faith.

Gittins, Anthony. *Gifts and Strangers: Meeting the Challenge of Inculturation.* New York: Paulist Press, 1989. Written from a missionary perspective, this accessible work is written especially for pastoral agents who minister in a cross-cultural context.

Groome, Thomas. "Inculturation: How to Processed in a Pastoral Context." In Greinacher and Mette, eds. *Christianity and Cultures. Concilium* 1994/2: 120–33. This noted expert on religious education offers a method known as "shared Christian praxis" that is easily applicable to a discussion of the inculturation of the liturgy.

Kress, Robert. "We the People: The American Transformation of Roman Catholicism from Established State Church to Voluntary Free Church." *New Theology Review* 6 (1993): 63–88. A fascinating discussion of the influence of U.S. culture on the Catholic church—for good and for ill. A good place to go for historical background on the topic.

Moore, R. Lawrence. *Selling God: American Religion in the Market-place of Culture*. New York: Oxford University Press, 1994. An engaging history of the gradual commercialization of religion in the United States, from Bible-based diet books *(More of Jesus and Less of Me)* to religious theme parks. There is much here for pastoral ministers to ponder as they discern the difference between responding to legitimate pastoral need and "giving the people what they want."

Schineller, Peter. *A Handbook of Inculturation*. New York: Paulist Press, 1990. This short, nontechnical approach to incultura-tion offers a fine way to begin a more systematic study of the process of inculturation in a pastoral setting. A good book to begin a general study of inculturation.

Schreiter, Robert. *Constructing Local Theologies*. Maryknoll, New York: Orbis Books, 1985. One of the most influential works on inculturation, this clearly-written book presents both the theory and practical implications of inculturation for local churches.

———. *The New Catholicity: Theology between the Global and the Local*. Maryknoll, New York: Orbis Books, 1998. This volume serves as a sequel to Schreiter's previous work and explores the wider panorama of globalization and how this phenome-non relates to contextualizing the faith.

Shorter, Aylward. *Toward a Theology of Inculturation*. Maryknoll, New York: Orbis Books, 1988. The author, a British priest, anthropologist and missionary in Africa presents a fine overview of the history of faith and culture from a Roman Catholic perspective, and a comprehensive treatment of the dynamic of inculturation, especially in an African context.

Liturgical Inculturation

Bernstein, Eleanor, ed. *Liturgy and Spirituality in Context: Perspectives on Prayer and Culture.* Collegeville, Minnesota: The Liturgical Press, 1990. This collection of essays by noted liturgists focuses on the relationship between liturgy and culture in the United States. Of special interest are essays by M. Francis Mannion, Mark Searle, John Baldovin and Robert Hovda, each of whom treat the topic of Catholic worship in contemporary U.S. culture.

Chupungco, Anscar. *Liturgical Inculturation: Sacramentals, Religiosity and Catechesis.* Collegeville, Minnesota: Liturgical Press, 1992. This internationally-respected expert on liturgical inculturation offers a systematic way of viewing the process of inculturating the liturgy, as well as a study of inculturation's relationship with popular religiosity and catechesis. A basic book for any Catholic approach to this topic.

————. *Worship: Sound Tradition and Legitimate Progress.* Washington, D.C.: The Pastoral Press, 1994. A collection of essays that focus on particular areas of liturgical inculturation: baptism, eucharist, music, multicultural worship. In many ways, these essays apply the principles enunciated in Chupungco's previous work.

Duffy, Regis. *An American Emmaus: Faith and Sacrament in the American Culture.* New York: Crossroad, 1995. Leading sacramental theologian Regis Duffy explores the "conversion walk" we in U.S. culture are invited to make in order to discover Christ in the context of our diverse culture.

Elizondo, Virgilio, and Matovina, Timothy. *Mestizo Worship: A Pastoral Approach to Liturgical Ministry.* Collegeville, Minnesota: The Liturgical Press, 1998. This collection of essays presents a Hispanic vision of liturgy and popular religion that is born from a sensitive listening to Mexican Americans and grounded in their experience of a faith lived in the midst of a community.

Francis, Mark. *Guidelines for Multicultural Celebrations*. Washington, D.C.: FDLC, 1998. These guidelines were commissioned by the Federation of Diocesan Liturgical Commissions as a revision and amplification of their 1987 guidelines. It includes a bibliography and discussion questions.

————. *Liturgy in a Multicultural Community.* Collegeville, Minnesota: The Liturgical Press, 1991. This primer for pastoral ministers deals with the basic issues involved in preparing liturgy in a multicultural context. Chapters dealing with faith, culture, and the history of the inculturation of the liturgy help to introduce the final chapter on pastoral/liturgical issues. An appendix includes the 1987 FDLC *Guidelines for Multilingual Masses;* the book also includes an annotated bibliography.

————. "Liturgical Inculturation: The State of the Question." *Liturgical Ministry* 6 (1997): 97–107. The author presents an overview of recent literature on liturgical inculturation by presenting various methods and points of view on the nature of inculturation, and the changes possible in the cultural adaptation of the rites. This article presupposes some familiarity with the topic.

Francis, Mark, and Pérez-Rodríguez, Arturo. *Primero Dios: Hispanic Liturgical Resource.* Chicago: Liturgy Training Publications, 1997. The authors use both exposition, story and sample rituals to discuss the place of Hispanic popular religious customs in inculturated celebrations of the rites of passage in Hispanic communities. This is an accessible book for those just beginning Hispanic liturgical ministry and interested in the question of culture.

Gaillardetz, Richard. "North American Culture and the Liturgical Life of the Church: The Separation of the Quests for Transcendence and Community." *Worship* 68 (1994): 403–16. Provocative analysis of what some feel is the current malaise in the American church with regard to liturgy, which the author locates in a "privatized quest for transcendence" that has undercut much of the potential of Vatican II's liturgical renewal.

Hoffman, Lawrence. "Liturgical Reform as Second Reformation," in *Sung Liturgy: Toward 2000 AD.* Virgil Funk, ed. Washington, D.C.: The Pastoral Press, 1991. Rabbi Hoffman provides an insightful history of the relationship of worship and culture in the United States from the period after World War II to the 1990s.

Mannion, M. Francis, "Liturgy and Culture: Part I. A Variety of Approaches." *Liturgy 80* 20 (April 1989): 4–6; "Part II," *Liturgy 80* 20 (July 1989): 2–5. An engaging presentation of the way that Catholics of the U.S. have responded to the challenge of liturgical inculturation. An excellent way to begin a parish discussion.

Secretariat for the Liturgy and Secretariat for Black Catholics, *Plenty Good Room: The Spirit and Truth of African American Catholic Worship.* Washington, D.C.: USCC, 1991. This is a basic resource for African American Catholic liturgy in the United States. Its exposition of the place of culture and the characteristics of African American Catholic worship are clearly written and pastorally sensitive.

Phan, Peter. "How Much Uniformity Can We Stand? How Much Do We Want? Church and Worship in the Next Millennium." *Worship* 72 (1998): 194–209. The author, a Vietnamese American priest and professor of religion and culture at Catholic University, Washington, D.C., offers a highly readable overview of many of the issues involved with inculturation of the liturgy.

Senn, Frank. *The Witness of the Worshiping Community.* New York: Paulist Press, 1993. This is a very readable overview of the issues surrounding the commercialization of worship as found in a "church growth" approach to liturgy. The author, a Lutheran pastor, offers a way of opening up the evangelizing potential of a community that truly is engaged in worship.